HOME IDEA
NOTEBOOK

HOME IDEA
NOTEBOOK

A DESIGN GUIDE FOR EVERY ROOM IN THE HOUSE

THUNDER BAY
P·R·E·S·S

Text and material on pages 8–297 appeared originally (in a slightly different form) in *Home Design Workbook*, copyright 1999, Rockport Publishers (design by Sawyer Design Associates, Inc.); *Designing Interiors with Tile*, copyright 2000, Rockport Publishers (design by Mimi Ahmed, Stephen Perfetto, Leeann Leftwich); *The New Wallpaper Book*, copyright 1999, Rockport Publishers (design by Elastic Design); *East West Style*, copyright 2000, Rockport Publishers (design by Kristen Webster, layout by SYP Design & Production); and *Big Ideas for Small Spaces*, copyright 2000, Rockport Publishers (design by Stoltze Design).

Photos on page 42: Ann Sacks Tile (top left); Artistic Tile (top right); Waterworks (bottom left); Kohler (bottom right).
Photos on page 43: Walker Zanger/Stuart Watson (top); Fired Earth (bottom).
Photos on page 44 (clockwise from top left): Tile: Ann Sacks Tile and Stone; Design: Marci Feigen; Photo: Paeter Ledwith. Tile: Bisazza; Photo: Eric Roth.
Photos on page 66: Gramercy (top); Sunworthy Wallcoverings (bottom).
Photos on page 67: Brunschwig & Fils (top); Village (bottom).
Photo on page 100: Steve Vierra.
Photos on page 101: Steve Vierra, interior design by Marian Glasgow (top); Paul Ferrino, interior design by Peter Forbes (bottom).

First published in 2001 by
Thunder Bay Press
An imprint of the Advantage Publishers Group
5880 Oberlin Drive, San Diego, CA 92121-4794
www.advantagebooksonline.com

Cover Image: Imperial Wallcoverings
Cover Design: Leeann Leftwich

ISBN 1-57145-684-8
Library of Congress Cataloging-in-Publication Data available upon request.

Printed in China.

1 2 3 4 5 01 02 03 04 05

Contents

Welcome

COMING HOME SHOULD FEEL LIKE GETTING A BIG HUG. When a room has been decorated successfully, simply walking in can warm the spirit and encourage lingering. In this way, good decorating is about making rooms "feel" as good as they look.

For so many of us with active lifestyles, our homes have evolved from mere shelters. They are now entertainment centers, work stations, and storage compounds for the warehousing of our lives. The physical demands on our housing are layered and growing, with design concerns from safe child-rearing to accommodating aging parents. So, too, are our attitudes about home decoration. New needs have made us full of fresh ideas on nesting.

Families are no longer mindlessly following home fashion trends and creating sterile "company-only" rooms in which our families can't relax. Instead, we are more interested in living in comfortable, organized, and secure homes that offer peace apart from the world. Over-decorating is a thing of the past. Simplicity is being rediscovered.

We are re-thinking the traditional uses of some rooms. For instance, making a bathroom into a spa can make some feel pampered. Dining rooms that double as daytime play space breathe life into long-barren spaces in many homes. Home decorators are inspired to explore and express their personalities. And comfort, most would agree, is perhaps the ultimate luxury.

Although interested in decorating, you may not be confident about where to begin, what will work and how to achieve the look you want.

This book illustrates the principles of putting together great rooms. This is a primer on how professionals and home owners have used basic knowledge of design—composition, balance, color, texture and personal flair—to create special spaces.

Coming home should feel like slipping under warm bedcovers. This canopied bed was tailored in cotton matelasse, with natural line bedcovers and dust skirt. The rough hewn plank flooring is set against a natural sisal rug, juxtaposing the rough material against fragile white cotton. INTERIOR DESIGN: WALKER DESIGN GROUP

9

Color that thrills you. Art that makes your heart glad. Flowers that give you joy. These are the small details that decorators use to create rooms that reflect the spirit of the people who live in them. So ask yourself, if you were a room, what color would you be? This living room was created from space reclaimed by a homeowner with a recently "emptied nest." The client wanted a comfortable room with abundant seating and bookcases to showcase their collectibles, art and family photos. INTERIOR DESIGN: RITA ST. CLAIR ASSOCIATES INC.

The key to professional looking results is to decorate your house in stages, starting with the bare walls and filling space according to your budget and needs. You will learn, as the great design professionals understand, that a room is never "completely" decorated; rooms can and should change as do our lives and interests.

This book fosters a no-fear attitude in those who worry that any mistake in color or furniture style is fatal or eternal. Also it encourages those who fancy the idea of being a "serial decorator"—working and re-working a space until they feel more at home in it.

In this book, you will learn to develop your own time-track and floor plan to fit your budget and your style of decoration.

It sets out some of the visual possibilities from the humble to the haute, offering something for every room in the house and providing a rich source of inspiration and instruction.

The chapters are arranged step-by-step. First is an inventory of who you are and what makes you feel at home. Next comes a brief course in interior-design basics, to help you begin to understand the relationships between everything in a room. Then we take a room apart, illustrating options for walls, floors, ceiling, windows, and entrances or hallways. Later chapters look at completed rooms.

Taken together, the four parts of this book will guide you through the process creating a space that reflects the essence of your individuality.

— B.H. Lawrence

Chapter 1

DESIGN FOR

Living

A ROOM SHOULD BE A REFUGE that calms you, pleases you and makes of you no demands. Great rooms begin with how you feel about being in them. Successful decorating involves making rooms feel as good as they look.

Whether you are decorating your first home or a temporary space, a home is really an attitude and a mind-set that is created physically by the choices you make. Your home should provide a sense of belonging.

Here, together, we will begin to discover how you reflect on your own aspirations to reveal what makes you feel at home. So before you even consider a swatch or paint chip, ask yourself "who do you want to be?"

The geography outside your home may inspire the decor inside. In the Southwest, for example, much of the architecture and the living habitats are designed to blend with the environment. This works indoors, as well. INTERIOR DESIGN: CAROL CONWAY DESIGN ASSOCIATES; PHOTO: MARK BOISCLAIR

Section 1

INSPIRATIONS FOR CHANGE

Your first thoughts
about decorating your
home should not
involve color,
cornices, or chintz.

You should think
about you.

What do you need
from your home?

Who are you when you
feel most "at home?"

WHO YOU ARE

If people could be divided into types, some might be said to enjoy stimulation such as auto-racing and skydiving, while others might prefer more relaxed outings—gazing upon sunsets on nearly deserted beaches, swims in mountain streams. So in thinking this way you might ask yourself: "Are you for racing or relaxing?"

Of course there are infinite variations on what makes you feel good at different times. But with this type of information about you and your living partners, you may begin to tailor your views about how to outfit and to decorate your home.

Design professionals always interview their clients about their lives, lifestyles and aspirations, long before they discuss issues of decorating. What you enjoy is as important as your choice of window dressings.

There are only subjective rules when it comes to decorating. Many confuse this fact by believing that there is a "right way" or a "right combination" to decorating a space. What is light and open to one may feel hollow and empty to another. What seems cozy and "lived-in" to another might seem cluttered and unsafe to you. Wherever you see yourself, what matters is the courage to work those realities into your design plans.

Even with full acceptance of the infinite range of individual tastes, there has evolved a vocabulary of proportion, arrangement and decorative practice that we can learn from.

The aim of this workbook is to simplify and direct your decision-making by getting you to look at your needs, your home and organize and to have a plan for creating the place where you'll feel at home.

What makes you feel at home? Being in a sunny window seat? A room such as this sunny nook might make home sweeter for you. INTERIOR DESIGN: BLAIR ASSOCIATES, INC.

Your home journal

Create a personal "Home" journal—as simple a document as folded paper or notecards—bind with a ribbon or rubber band and fill with your written thoughts of who you think you are and what makes you feel most at home. You may want to allow everyone who lives with you to make a version of this type of journal, depending on how much you'd value their comments. You may store this journal along with bits of images and objects that have made you comfortable. For example, the smooth, glass-like rocks you collect along the shore could ultimately provide the inspiration for the type of flooring or color you'd like to use in your home.

THINGS THAT MAKE YOU FEEL AT HOME

Home is where we should feel at ease. And for most of us, the significance of "home" is far deeper than the accumulation of all our possessions under one roof. We should seek to create surrounding that convey this sense.

We are affected by the many places in which we spend our lives, often without being aware of it. Usually, when we want to improve our mental well-being, we try to alter our relationships and our emotional framework. We should also consider altering our physical surroundings to improve our psychological life. The idea of encouraging harmony between humans and our surroundings is a cornerstone of most of the world's major philosophies and religions. Designers today encourage decorators to consider furnishings and colors that they like so that the time in the room will be more enjoyable. So decorating involves all the senses, not only sight but smell, sound, touch and even taste.

Image a walk alone on a beach. Now contrast this with an image of walking through Broadway in New York City's midtown at rush hour. Calm and chaos. Your rooms can be designed to help create a "feeling," what design professionals and sociologists call "a sense of place." The role of the senses should play into your decorating and design decisions.

A place to start is by making a list of some of the houses, rooms or hotels or any room or space where you've felt good. Don't worry about the reason it made you feel good. Daydream about places in your past where you've felt comfortable and record the important thoughts. The earthy smell of your grandmother's garden. The light in the window of the church you attend. The point of this analysis is to reveal what images, tastes, smells, sights move you.

Once you have an idea about who you are and where you're going, getting to your ideal "home" is a relatively straight route.

Which styles attract you? What colors are you moved by? A golden master suite, spare yet elegant, serves as a retreat in this Palm Beach home. INTERIOR DESIGN: STEDILA DESIGN, INC.

WHERE YOU LIVE

If you are at home, take a good look around you. Do you feel at home with what you see? Do you hate that sofa? Do you hate the way the newspapers collect right by the door and always spill over before trash day? Do you love the way the morning light streams into your bedroom window or the sound of rain on the attic's skylight?

After you have explored your current response to your living space, you should look at where you live now and who lives with you. You should make a list of the positive and negative aspects of the space and its furnishings as well as assessing the structural needs of your home.

To create the necessary detachment for this exercise, you might consider yourself a visitor or a would-be tenant or home-buyer.

Begin outside. Do you like the way you enter your home? Are there obstructions that impede you or are there visual irritants? These are comfort as well as design issues. Note them all for future reference. (You can never be "too critical" in this assessment stage.)

Continue your analysis room by room; include the hallways and "dead spaces" too. Are there spaces that you'd be embarrassed to show to another? Why? Ask yourself the questions about the plumbing, structure and maintenance needs. After you've looked at where you live now, think about how you'd like to live and what changes are needed.

Are you ready for change? This garage was converted into a sunny family room when there was no longer a need to house two cars. Interior Design: Trilogy

WORKBOOK

CONDUCTING YOUR PERSONAL INVENTORY

To help you assess your personal and home decor needs, the questions below will suggest the areas you need to think about. You will learn how to work with this information in later chapters.

1. Who lives here and what space and taste needs do they have? (Elderly relatives, toddlers, and pets have different needs, but all can be accommodated if considered during the planning stages.)

2. Which rooms are used most? Do they have multiple uses?

3. What are your storage needs?

4. What do you most like and dislike about your apartment or house?

5. How do you move around the house? Are there unused doors and entrances? Are there bottlenecks?

6. Where does clutter accumulate despite organization efforts?

INTERIOR DESIGN: LILIAN BOGOSSIAN AND VIVIAN WEIL, DECORATIVE INTERIORS
PHOTO: STEVE VIERRA

7. In which rooms do you feel most comfortable? Why?

8. In which rooms do family and friends naturally congregate?

9. Can you comfortably entertain? How many? For how long?

10. How's your lighting?

11. Are surfaces and finishes practical where they need to be—in the kitchen, bathrooms, or children's room?

Who should you call if you need help?

If you'd like decorating help but think it may be out of your price range, you may want to shop around. Designers can help with any aspect of the project from planning the space to helping you select a chaise. If you have special concerns where you feel you need a trained designer, you may shop around for price and personality that you're comfortable with. The designer should take you through this same process of self-analysis, planning, budget, and execution. Prices for interior design services average about $125 an hour through the industry, although designers set their own rates. The American Society of Interior Designers and the Organization of Black Designers, both headquartered in Washington, D.C., offer worldwide referral services and will, at no charge, suggest design professionals in your area.

ARE YOU READY FOR CHANGE?

Decorating is not something that everyone approaches eagerly, but we should welcome change. Whether you are re-designing your old house or decorating one from scratch, change should be made only after you've assessed yourself and your needs.

Consider how you use rooms. Many of us are conventional when it comes to assigning uses to rooms. However, we do have choices in what functions we assign spaces. Your toddlers may need the play space that is now the dining room, especially if the room stands unused except for holidays.

You may choose to alter your impression of a room by re-arranging the elements that are already there—arranging the furniture or hanging the pictures differently. Your feelings of comfort and being "at home" will grow with time, as you juggle and refine different elements until everything feels right. Few really successful or interesting rooms are created in a weekend. They grow in complexity and texture.

WHERE TO START

Design professionals offer three words to remember when beginning a decorating plan: Budgeting, purging, and patience.

Don't start out to decorate your whole home. It's too big a project and you'll end up frustrated. Unless you have a budget that would allow sweeping changes throughout, the most satisfying approach is to plan your decoration in stages.

Budgeting

Money is probably the biggest determining factor in any decorating plan. The first step is figuring out what you can afford. Large-scale projects that require renovations need more money than updating a decorating scheme does.

If you're working within a budget, work out a stage-by-stage plan. Begin by planning what changes you'd like to make. You have already determined through your personal analysis what you'd like to have at home. Decide what you must do now and what you would like to do in the future.

Now you can begin a realistic assessment of what you have to work with. Some of the most immediate and far-reaching changes you can make to your home have to do with its organization. A new layout can conjure up new space and transform confusion into calm.

What period of furnishings or artwork are you attracted to? This may become your inspiration around which to decorate.

Interior Design: James R. Irving, ASID

Create your very own style file

Design professionals encourage clients to collect visual representations of what they have in mind. Collect swatches of fabrics, samples of wallpaper and pictures of rooms from magazines that attract your attention. Sort through your collection, analyzing different elements. Do this often enough and you will see similarities among the decorating themes you like. Note them and store them in the "hope chest."
Your daydreams may reveal a lot to help you in developing a decorating plan. This is a lesson in visual perception. When you're pouring over images and ideas about how you would like to live at home, take notes. Imagine how your fantasy home will look and record that in your journal or your Style File.

Paring Down

Many of us end up sharing our lives with unwanted and useless objects because we can't work out what to do with them or we lack the nerve. "Have nothing in your houses that you do not know to be useful or believe to be beautiful," was designer William Morris's golden rule.

Teach yourself to evaluate everything you own. Do you really like it? If you "kind of" like something, dump it. If you like it, why? What does it contribute to the way you want to live? Exercise the same critical approach to new possessions. Of course, before you begin trashing shared possessions, consider others living with you. The emotions involved in creating a home and living with other people's stuff are sometimes tangled.

Some women think men are not interested in the way the house looks, but some may be. Legendary decorator Elsie de Wolfe said, "It is the personality of the mistress that the home expresses. Men are forever guests in our homes. . .." But it is also said, "a man's home is his castle" and this must include the trappings. If you are a couple, approach this purging stage as a couple.

When possessions begin to overwhelm you, it's time to rethink how and why you hang on to certain objects and to examine how you might find new room for storage.

Organizing your home probably won't take major structural overhauls—although as rule of thumb you always need at least twice as much storage space as you think you do. Organization professionals (you can find them in the phone book) specialize in helping people order their possessions, either concentrating on small pieces (such as only closets), or being all-encompassing. Interior designers can also address storage dilemmas. But with discipline and a specific point of view, you and your family can purge your possessions and uncover hidden storage space.

You must become creative in finding storage in your approach to home organization. Good storage and home organization means that you look at all the items you possess, and at how often, when, and why you use them (if at all). Then you may begin to store them where it makes sense and you'll know where to find them. Finding a place for needed items can save time and make chores and activities at home less stressful.

The repetition of cream-colored fabrics creates a subtly elegant and relaxing mood for this bedroom. INTERIOR DESIGN: C. WEAKS INTERIORS, INC.

Patience

The challenge in decorating your new home is likely to be both emotional and physical. Take your time in making your choices and selecting your new possessions. Do not feel pressured to buy impulsively just "to fill in a space." Designers say go slow: It's your home you're building, not a showroom.

Most of us fret if our rooms are not completely decorated. But a little patience and you will see how rooms can "grow" and fill in, and with objects you really like to live with.

Your time table for executing this plan should be tailored to your decorating budget and living needs. Follow the same steps whether you're able to complete the task in months or years. By doing so, you will be able to make more informed choices about what you'd like to like with at home. With an orderly decorating plan, you may end up with rooms in three stages. For example:

1. Your first stage of a decorating plan might leave you with a room that looks "minimalist" with just the objects and furnishings you have after you've edited the excess possessions, worked through your floor plan, and understand your space needs.

2. The second stage comes when you decide what additional pieces and changes you need to function better in your space. Most likely, this is when the room will begin to take on a more-full look as you've added your fabrics and wall and window treatments.

3. The final stage is a slow evolution that takes place when you start adding the decorative touches and personalizing it with the mementos of your life. This stage can continue indefinately.

The modern style furnishings in this dining space conveys a sense of lean, futuristic surroundings. Interior Design: Gayle Shaw Camden; Photo: Balthazar Korab

WHAT MOVES YOU?

Inspiration is the starting point for a decorating plan, and this first step is always the hardest. How do you go about finding out what seems right for you? What chair will comfort you and keep you in the right spirit?

Now that you've assessed yourself, your life, and your aspirations, you should feel more comfortable exploring how others have translated their imaginings into real rooms. You may now begin your exercises in visual perception. This means finding out what you're attracted to and why by looking at how some rooms have been put together.

Look at rooms you find appealing—rooms in other people's houses, in stores, in showhouses, in books and magazines, on television, and in films. Take in every part of the room from its structure to its decorative details. Study the rooms for how they come together. But don't seek to duplicate the design in your own home—look for the spirit of the room and use your own choices to bring that look together. It is worth spending time to discover what appealed to you and why so you will have clear ideas to help you create your special look.

Whether the idea of what the room should be or the actual furniture choices comes first, having something to say is the only prerequisite to putting together a great room. Many elements are involved, so you should have by now narrowed down your point of view. You should begin to see a familiarity among the images and items that appeal to you, whether in the furniture style, the color combinations, the furniture itself, or the lack of it.

Here you can begin to learn the vocabulary of the styles and palettes you're interested in so you may become a more-informed consumer and investigator of your decorative options. For example, you may be interested in chinoiserie patterns on walls and fabrics or lacquered surfaces, a design category loosely called "Oriental style."

In another area, you may discover that you are attracted to rooms because of what is left out rather than what is included. Your ideal home may involve a spare or "minimalist" approach to decor. You may find that you and your family will be comfortable in nearly empty spaces, and that the basic qualities of the light and air are more important than the look of your home.

Family antiques and warm colors create
a cozy, personal atmosphere in this
space suitable for casual or fine dining.

INTERIOR DESIGN: GAIL ADAMS INTERIORS LTD.

WORK OUT A STAGE BY STAGE PLAN FOR CHANGE.

It is important to assess and evaluate your existing belongings in order to discover what you need. These questions will help you create a specific plan of action.

PHOTO COURTESY OF: CRATE & BARREL

1. What changes would you like to make?

2. What changes can you afford to make?

3. What changes do you plan for the future?

4. Do you really like the furniture you have?

5. If you like it, why?

6. What does it contribute to the way you want to live?

....

....

....

....

7. What kind of space do you have to work with?

....

....

....

....

8. How much and what types of furniture do you already have that you want to keep?

....

....

....

....

....

....

Chapter 2

Begin

CREATING A ROOM THAT LOOKS AND feels good is not a mysterious process. The point is not to get it right by adhering to rules or following fashion, but rather to find what you like and incorporate it.

When putting together a room, start by understanding a few principles of composition that professionals use: space, color, pattern, light, and texture.

Space is the essential defining quality of a room. How much is there? How little? What is the quality of the space? Space is used as part of the decorative statement in this modern dining space where the architecture is highlighted with lighting and light palettes on walls, ceilings and the floor. INTERIOR DESIGN: ENVIRONMENTS BY MARILYN FRANCES LUNDY

Section 1

SPACE

Part of this phase
of your decorating
plan is to gain a
basic understanding
of how to use what
space you have.

Drama on a dime

Large rooms will seem more intimate if
you light them with table lamps,
uplights, and well-placed spots.

SPACE IS THE REAL VALUE OF A DWELLING, not the decor. You should explore the dimensions, shape and quality of your existing spaces. You may have lived there for a number of years, but do you really understand how the space works, how each room relates to the others in terms of scale, shape and orientation? This assessment process provides you with a concrete framework in which to test your ideas.

You need a floor plan to determine how to use the space and whether all your possessions will fit. Getting all the measurements down on paper will give you a much clearer picture of your home's space and proportions. Most of our space considerations have to do with creating more of it, or at least the illusion of it. Decorators use a few visual tricks to "make space" or to make a room seem more or less than what it is.

Storing possessions will create more real space. Room by room, consider all storage options, including wall-mounted, units, freestanding stacking systems such as crates or baskets, or prefabricated space-saving systems that can be custom fit to your needs. Also consider less-expensive storage devices, including canvas shelving for more organized closets. Don't forget to look into the so-called "dead space" under floor areas and stairs for possibly useful space.

Mirrors are a decorator's magic wand when it comes to changing perceptions about a room's space. Placed strategically, mirrors create the illusion of more space than there is. A wall of mirrors, used from floor to ceiling, will the give the impression of at least double the actual space. (Curtains on either side will create the illusion of an arch leading into a second room.)

A mirrored panel between two windows will give the illusion of a whole wall of windows, especially if the mirror is the same size as the windows. Mirrored panels cut to size of a room's windows, then framed and hung on the opposite wall, will give the impression that there are windows on both sides of the room and will reflect extra light.

If a mirror is used to create a complete illusion, its edges should not show. The mirror should run to the very edge of the wall, up to a doorjamb or out of sight behind curtains. If the mirror must stop where the edges can be seen, disguise them by framing them or using a decorative trim.

A fireplace defines the space, while custom shelving gives variety and textures to the walls. INTERIOR DESIGN: MICHAEL C.F. CHAN & ASSOCIATES INC.

How to Make a Floor Plan of Your Home:

A. Sketch a rough diagram of each floor or room, showing the approximate shape and size together with any connecting hallways, and the position of the doors, windows and fixtures such as fireplaces, alcoves, radiators and closets.

B. With a tape measure, measure the length and width of each room, including the sizes of fixtures such as chimneys and alcoves. Measure the thickness of walls or partitions, the width of doorways and windows, and the dimensions of built-in fixtures such as kitchen units. Transfer each measurement to the appropriate position on the floor plan.

C. Determine the function for each room, whether that is for eating, relaxing or bathing.

D. Cover the floor plan with a sheet of tracing paper and then start drawing in the basic elements, bearing in mind the size of each item in relation to its room. Will everything fit? Add to the floor plan your storage areas or storage requirements as well at this point.

E. With the list of possessions you created in your Chapter One inventory, begin to fill in your floor plan and toy with possible positions. The list should include all the furniture, appliances, and objects that require floor space that you wish to include in the room and their measurements.

F. Expect to repeat Step D because you will probably have to experiment and create many versions of your floor plan until you discover a solution. Do not be discouraged. With planning, despite any space limitations you perceive, your possessions can likely be arranged to create a workable, livable home. A floor plan provides you with an excellent view without moving the furniture.

G. Once you have a livable plan, check your measurements. Now photocopy your completed floor plan and your measurements and store them.

Graph paper is provided in the back of this book so that you can make a floor plan of your home.

Living in one room:

There may be more space than you think.

If you are living in a studio or loft, here are some ideas and questions to ask yourself:

1. Do you want to keep the room as open as possible, or would you prefer to divide it into several smaller areas? Is there a change of level or is it possible to create one?

2. Are there items of furniture that may be used as focal points or for screening? Screens can be mysterious as well as practical.

3. Examine your sleeping options. Can the sofa bed or futon be put away in a hurry? Does it dominate? You could opt for a bed that remains on view but this limits your social options (save the screens).

4. Daybeds can be used for both sleeping and seating and they may be placed against a wall or in the center of a room.

5. You may elect to create room dividers. Lengths of fabrics or blinds hung from a ceiling make effective room dividers and they can be tied back or easily opened. Use plenty of fabric for a generous visual effect.

In a space with a given focal point such as this stone fireplace, the furnishings should be kept spare so as not to compete. PHOTO: ROBERT PERRON

COLOR/PATTERN

Certain colors excite us, others relax us.

Some lift our moods while others depress us.

Color has proven to have such a powerful effect on people that it is used therapeutically.

In addition to altering your moods, effective use of color can compensate for negative factors such as lack of natural light or ill-proportioned spaces.

WHICH HUES DO WHAT FOR YOU?

Color is one of the most emotional subjects in decorating and is very, very personal. These are some widely accepted notions about our emotional and cultural associations with certain colors. You may or may not feel the same as others about each hue.

Blue: The shade of sea and sky, blue is thought to induce calm. But blues can also be rich and vibrant, and too much blue can make a room seem cold. In its deepest tone, blue becomes purple, the color of royalty.

Green: Because of its association with freshness and nature, green evokes a restful, secure feeling. Greens work well in bedrooms and living rooms.

Yellow: The color of sunshine and summer days, yellow lifts the spirits. The brightest color in the spectrum, yellow can be either hot or cold depending on the amount of red it contains. Combined with red, yellow becomes orange, associated with happiness and power.

Red: Red has powerful, primitive associations with daring and passion and has been proven to increase the heart rates in some who view it. In small doses, red can be rich and opulent. In its lighter hues of pink, it evokes feelings of pure romance and innocence. Pinks and red-peachy hues are good choices for dressing areas and baths because the reflected color tends to flatter all skin tones.

Neutrals: Restrained, neutral schemes are quiet. Based on blends of grays, browns, greens, or yellow, the naturally occurring tones found in the earth, in wood and in stone, neutrals introduce an organic feel.

White: Associated with innocence and purity, white can create peaceful and relaxing interiors. It is easy to use because it mixes well with all colors and seems to enlarge small spaces. For kitchens, white is thought to be the best color because it shows off the color of the foods and conveys a sense of cleanliness.

Brown: A color with a heavy feel, associated with earth and therefore stability and solid ground, brown can be quite elegant and restful if balanced with a lighter tone.

Black: Black carries with it feelings of depth in mood and perspective. It can convey a lack of hope and therefore can depress, but in moderation black lends an air of sophistication and openness.

Gray: Gray is for some a gloomy shade. To some who don't enjoy cloudy days, it conjures up feelings of frustration. For others, gray is a balance between black and white and resolution of conflict—a perfect neutral.

Tradition has taught us that only certain colors are appropriate for certain spaces, so we tend to follow by rote, sticking with certain shades and shying away from using strong colors. But when coloring your world, have no fear: The rules are few and the rewards are many.

If living with color is new to you, selecting a palette can leave you befuddled. Look back to your style file to learn what colors you enjoy. Even if you don't have a "favorite" color, you'll be instinctively drawn to one a family of colors, which keep cropping up in your clothes and possessions.

When deciding a color scheme for a room, consider what furnishings and art pieces will be used there. Richly patterned fabrics can give good ideas for color schemes, as can china and ceramic art. Even if you decide to play it safe and begin with a neutral background, you can experiment with color in furnishings. Don't worry if your existing furniture doesn't match your new color choices. Creating a pulled-together room doesn't mean everything has to match. Mixing things up is more interesting. There are no rules when it comes to mixing colors—it is largely a matter of personal taste.

Avoid clashes over color

When professionals advise couples at this stage of decorating, they advise that each person contribute ideas and suggestions for palettes. Generally speaking, the husband will have one favorite color and the wife another. Combine the two, use white as a third color, and you have a color palette to use in choosing colors for walls, floors, and windows.

Check this out

One of the easiest ways of using pattern is as a decorative focal point, such as a patterned rug as the centerpiece of room.

Familiar patterns

- **Florals:** Among the most popular and versatile patterns, florals lend a soft, romantic atmosphere.

- **Geometrics:** Stripes and checks are timeless patterns. On fabrics they work well when paired with florals. Stripes can be sophisticated on wallpaper. Checkerboard lends a country spirit. African-inspired patterns lend spirit of heritage.

WHAT IS COLOR? HOW TO USE A COLOR WHEEL

There are three primary colors: red, yellow and blue. Every other color is a mixture of these three, with either white or black added. Colors can be represented in a circle called a color wheel that allows you to see how colors work together. For example, purple "works well" with blue because they sit side by side on the color wheel—that is, they are harmonious and tend to blend well together. Colors that sit opposite each other (but still work well together) are called complementary. For example, purple and yellow sit opposite each other on the color wheel. Study a color wheel to get a feel of the range and the compatibility of certain colors.

If you want to begin your color palette with your favorite color, choose it as your dominant color and then use the complementary or harmonious color as your accent color.

The natural world may be your best teacher of what colors go best together. Many of the best color partnerships draw their inspiration from nature: a yellow sunflower against a blue summer sky, or green moss covering a brown tree trunk. After all, Mother (Nature) knows best.

COLOR BLIND? VISUAL TRICKS USING COLOR

Colors can affect the way we see a space, so consider a color's overall impact on a room, taking into account the amount of natural or artificial lighting as well as the mood you seek.

1. Intense, warm colors such as yellows, reds, and oranges advance, making objects seem closer.

2. Blues, greens, grays, and purples recede, seeming to open up space.

3. A room without any architectural detailing can be enlivened if one wall is painted a different color than the others.

4. Light, airy colors make rooms look bigger.

5. To "lower" a high ceiling, try painting it two or three shades darker than the walls.

6. To "raise" a low ceiling, use a pale, cool color.

7. Painting the end wall of a narrow room in a strong color will make it appear wider and nearer.

Pattern, with color, is one of the most basic design tools. No matter how subtle, patterns can bring a room to life adding character, depth and visual interest. It can be used to define, as in a border of checkered tile work, or to provide an accent and focus, as in a rich Oriental rug in a modern space. Consider using a pattern to unify. Pick a pattern that you (and your family) feel good about—florals, stripes, checks—and consider using variations on it everywhere, from fabrics to flooring and walls to window dressings. Scale is important in using pattern. Large patterns jump out at you. Small ones recede.

Profusions of patterns are not for the faint-hearted. Some patterns demand attention, and others are subtle. In general, bold, insistent patterns need to be complemented by muted surfaces. Quiet, small-scale patterns mix more readily. Most checks and stripes are the pattern equivalent of neutral shades and combine well, both with each other and with other patterns. They usually work best in regularly shaped rooms, where they give a sense of graphic definition and help emphasize the room's shape.

To mix other patterns, look for a common denominator, such as color, theme, or scale. You will find groups of prints that mix well in the same way.

A profusion of pattern is not for faint-h
In this sunny sitting room, the pattern
tied together by being taken from the
color family. INTERIOR DESIGN: CHAMBERS INTERIORS AND ASSOCIATES INC.

C O L O R

A N D

P A T T E R N

W I T H

TILES

F or centuries, ceramic tile makers experimented to broaden the range of colors they could achieve, subjecting different colors of clay and mineral glazes to the alchemy of the kiln. Modern chemistry and production technologies have added new shades as well as new ways of achieving gradations of color within a single tile.

The highest of high-tech methods are applied to imitate the look and touch of ancient handmade tiles. New raw materials have replaced substances such as lead that were used in the past but are today considered environmentally sensitive. Today, manufacturers may subject a tile to more than twenty separate decorating procedures—painting, brushing, spattering—to duplicate the beauty and subtle variations in color and texture produced by the presence of lead in a glaze. From electric brights to soft neutrals, the ever-widening range of tile colors that found favor in the early 1990s is more complex today, enriched by nuanced mixtures and muted midtones. New techniques produce metallic, opalescent, and iridescent finishes, while faux stone is made in all the natural pinks, greens, grays, and golds of marble and granite. The popularity of multicultural influence is reflected in a world of imported ethnic tiles—earthy Mexican terra-cottas, exuberant Portuguese colors, classic Dutch blues and whites, elaborate Moroccan patterns. At the millennium, our attention is turned to the past; historic tiles of every period and style are being reproduced by manufacturers and tile artists alike.

Choosing and using color in interior design can establish a mood, arouse or calm the emotions, and evoke a particular style of living or historic era. This chapter explores the use of color in a variety of rooms, in a variety of distinctive expressions.

(above) Create an intricate multicolored tile rug to liven up an entry-way. Mix ceramic with mosaic in concentric circles and free yourself to accepting the decor possibilities. Tile: Illahe Tileworks; Design and Installation: Susan S. Werschkul; Photo: Patricia Bean. **(right) Give a bathroom a cool, back-to-nature texture and mood with garden-green tile walls finished with a leaf border and accenting terra-cotta stone tile floors.** Tile: ICT, Inc.; Tile Design: Talavera de Mexico; Interior Design: Susan Baker, Houston; Photo: Jack Thompson; Home: Susannah and David Schorlemer, Houston.

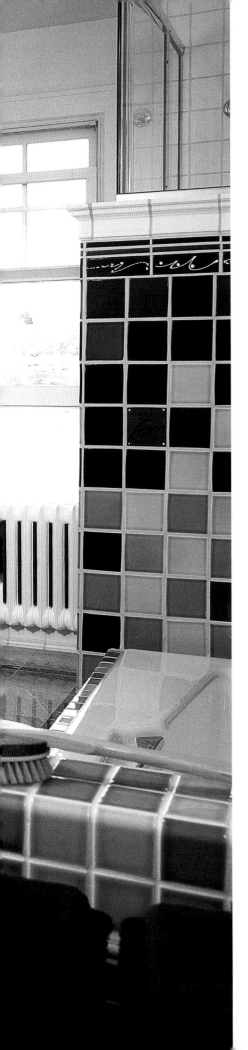

Plan carefully to successfully combine seven kinds of tile and stone. Notice how clusters of colors draw the eye around this bathroom and that some of the small wall tiles sport question marks, circles, or letters—a humorous touch. The tile that caps and finishes the wall catches the attention with shorthand squiggles. Finally, the high-gloss marble floor keeps the room feeling cool and clean. Photo: Stephen Cridland.

(above) Transform a low-light work area into a rainbow of color with tile. Photo: Tim Street-Porter. **(right) For people who need help waking up in the morning, install a sunrise of tile in an array of energizing shades. This cheery bath also features a wall of glass tile; peer through, and the colored tiles take on kaleidoscopic patterns and shapes.** Photo: Tim Street-Porter.

(left) Consider using repeating tile murals as if they were wallpaper. They can brighten a corner in need of color or an entire room, and they can form a rich backdrop for furniture, fabric, and art. Tile: Walker Zanger; Photo: Stuart Watson.

(above) Create a patchwork of art tiles, as the owners of this Houston home did, by piecing together a variety of traditional, century-old Spanish Talavera tile patterns rather than building an interlocking pattern or border with just one. Tile: ICT, Inc.; Tile Design: Talavera de Mexico; Interior Design: Susan Baker, Houston; Photo: Jack Thompson; Home: Susannah and David Schorlemer, Houston.

(right and opposite) **Set a tranquil mood with a wall of soft moss-green tiles. For a functional, stylish bathroom, add elegant details like frosted glass shelving, accents of silver, and engaging wide-rimmed vessel sinks. Complement blonde woods and simple platform countertops with textural, earth-toned floor tiles.** Tiles: Kohler Company; Design: Cynthia Leibrock and Eva Maddox Design.

Place tile to provide visual clues to utilitarian functions. In this bathroom, the checkerboard of yellow and white tile leads to the tub. Mixing small tiles with larger ones, and varying their shapes and colors, adds to the room's overall interest. Photo: Stephen Cridland.

Introduce vivid tile colors to your fireplace and create a focal point for a room. This Long Island getaway has color as its theme. Design: Charles Riley; Photo: Philip H. Ennis Photography.

(left) Consider designing your own trompe l'oeil tile rug to add color to a dark kitchen or break up a monochromatic floor.
Tile: Tile By Design; Photo: Leonard Myszynski. **(above) You can use color to take you to another time and place. The walls of this powder room were covered in a soft, pink-glazed ceramic tile in order to create a glamorous hideaway—the kind a starlet from the 40s might retreat to for a long bath. The designer of this luxurious room chose this pink tile for its sense of "Old World textural sexiness, and because it's effective at creating a sense of age."** Tile: California Art Tile, Pacific Design Center, Kohler Company; Interior Design: Mark Enos; Photo: David Glomb.

(opposite and above) Italian terra cotta and ceramic tiles in vibrant colors totally energize a room. The design lesson here is that you can use tile to warm up, cool down, or feel as though you're sipping morning tea in Tuscany. Tile: Bardelli, Cerasarda, and Il Pavone, Italy; Tile Design: Michael R.Golden Design; Interior Design: Carol Helms, *Garden Design Magazine*; Photos: Andre Baranowski.

(above) Go all out with gorgeous iridescent tiles that look as though they've been shaken off the wings of butterflies. Complete the look with crystal sink cradled on what appears to be a floating silver tray. This is drama at it's best. Tile: Kohler Company. (right) Choose a soft green cover of tile for a bath overlooking a flowering garden. The combination of greens, indoors and out, makes for a relaxing atmosphere in which to soak. Interior Design: Frank Fitzpatrick; Photo: Tim Street-Porter.

WALLCOVERINGS

AND COLOR

2

Sensational Style

A WELL-DECORATED ROOM with coordinating wallcoverings,
borders, and fabrics is no longer a luxury few can afford, nor need it be
a time-consuming effort of search and despair.

A wonderful world of decorating freedom has emerged. No longer is using stripes and prints together likely to produce raised eyebrows. One can even throw plaid fabrics into the mix. What makes it work? Primarily, color coordination. When the same colors are in the stripe, print, and plaid, interior style *works*.

One need not have the finely honed instincts of an interior designer to create striking style. Wallcovering companies have made coordinating easy by mixing and matching suggested patterns for you. As you leaf through their selection books, you will find colorful pages showing rooms in which coordinating prints have been applied on walls and ceilings, followed by samples of the actual wallcoverings used. These selection books can give an inspiring look at how to work with various patterns. Oftentimes, fabrics that match are available, adding to the wide range of customized interiors one can realize. A local seamstress can produce a stunning window treatment to mix with or match the patterns you select; coordinated comforters and bed linens can be created; and an upholstery shop can revamp existing furniture into stylish "new" pieces by recovering them with a fabric that echoes the pattern used on the walls or elsewhere in the room.

It is possible to create your own coordinated decor. While browsing through wallcovering selection books, look for the same color within the patterns, or colors of different *values* from within the same color family. Value refers to the lightness or darkness of a color achieved by tinting or shading. A *tint* is achieved by adding **white**, while a *shade* is achieved by adding **black** to a given color. For a good example of this concept, take a look at the strips of gradational colors available in paint stores. The lightest tinted color is at the top, while the deepest shaded color is at the bottom. Using a tint and a shade, one as dominant and the other as an accent or trim color, will result in good color coordination. Use the same principle of color value to guide you in selecting wallcovering patterns.

Mixed and matched wallcoverings can be used with one pattern on the upper half of a wall and the other on the lower half with a wooden chair rail or a wallcovering border to separate the patterns. Or use a dominant pattern on three walls with a coordinated pattern on the fourth. A dormered room can be papered with a dark background pattern on its walls and the same pattern, but in reverse (oftentimes available), within the dormers. The lighter reverse background will produce more reflected light.

The Feeling of Color

Here, color is broken down into families based around the same basic hue.

THE *RED* FAMILY

HUES
pink, rose, cardinal, raspberry, burgundy, maroon

CHARACTERISTICS
warmest of all colors, advancing, cheerful, active, stimulating, bold, vital, dramatic, exciting

EFFECT
A red room appears smaller by bringing the background closer; red objects appear larger because red focuses attention; red brings warmth and excitement to a cool room.

PRECAUTION
Too much red is overly exciting.

FAST FACT
A red room stimulates appetite.

·

THE *ORANGE* FAMILY

HUES
peach, coral, pumpkin, copper, terra-cotta, rust, warm brown

CHARACTERISTICS
welcoming, cheerful, warm, glowing, advancing, friendly

EFFECT
Much like the red family but to a lesser degree; in soft tints is a good color mixer; a good choice for kitchens and family rooms.

PRECAUTION
Like red, can be overwhelming if overused.

FAST FACT
Orange rooms tend to make people tire more easily.

THE *YELLOW* FAMILY

HUES
cream, straw, lemon, canary, gold, tan, tobacco

CHARACTERISTICS
warm, luminous, radiant, classic, expansive, accepting

EFFECT
Yellow rooms appear brighter and lighter because of the color's reflective quality; can be used to light up a room without making it feel smaller; a classic kitchen choice.

PRECAUTION
Yellow tints and tones need to be tested under artificial light as they appear different in various kinds of light.

FAST FACT
Babies tend to cry more and children are more argumentative in yellow nurseries than in pink, baby blue, or pale green rooms.

·

THE *GREEN* FAMILY

HUES
mint, lettuce, pea, grass, sea, olive, bottle, forest

CHARACTERISTICS
refreshing, cool, receding, restful

EFFECT
In lighter shades, a room will seem larger because the wall seems further away; brings atmosphere of relaxation to room; important hue where restfulness is important; most friendly with all other colors.

PRECAUTION
May make a room with a northern exposure feel cold.

FAST FACT
Green is least tiring to the eyes, which is the reason accountants' shades and surgeons' traditional scrubs are green.

·

THE *BLUE* FAMILY

HUES
baby, powder, sky, turquoise, royal, navy, midnight

CHARACTERISTICS
coolest of all colors, most receding, much-loved hue, serene

EFFECT
Blue room appears cooler than if painted with a warm hue; makes a room feel more airy and spacious; makes objects look smaller and more distant; makes whites appear more luminescent.

PRECAUTION
Can be depressing in dull shades.

FAST FACT
People associate stability and leadership with the color blue; important documents are often bound in blue.

THE *VIOLET* FAMILY

HUES

orchid, lavender, mauve, violet, purple, plum

CHARACTERISTICS

impressive hue; creates quiet feeling atmosphere

EFFECT

Dark tones make objects appear formal and rich; transitional color—feels cool when mixed with blue and warm when mixed with red; meditative.

PRECAUTION

Strong shades can be overpowering.

FAST FACT

In medieval times, only royalty was allowed to wear purple.

PRECEDING SPREAD: *As minimalism becomes more popular, we are likely to see patterns that fit the look.* IMPERIAL WALLCOVERINGS

ABOVE: *Older homes often have interesting architectural details such as the arched window and the built-in cabinet beside the fireplace. This appropriate wallcovering captures the spirit of the early twentieth century.* GRAMERCY

BELOW: *A traditional foyer sets the tone for a home. Don't be afraid to use rich colors; this red, for example, suggests warmth and cheerfulness.* SCHUMACHER

LEFT: *In this authentic bath, a botanical print wallcovering was used. Botanical prints were popular in the early part of this century. Good reproductions, such as this pedestal sink and footed bathtub, are now available for tho[se] wishing to capture the look.* GRAMERCY

BELOW: *A different pattern of wallcoveri[ng] helps to differentiate the alcove space from the rest of the room.* SEABROOK WALLCOVERING[S]

ABOVE: *Although we often associate red with oriental motifs, this blue with a subtle fish design works wonderfully with the decor.*
GRAMERCY

RIGHT: *A very charming eating area with a great deal of coordination. Everything matches to create a harmonious mood.* HARLEQUIN—
DISTRIBUTED BY WHITTAKER & WOODS

FACING PAGE: *This morning glory patt* *was a good choice as background to the bird* *house collection.* SEABROOK WALLCOVERING

LEFT: *A simple, Regency-inspired interior* *which the crispness of blue and white have bee* *used for a chic effect.* HARLEQUIN— DISTRIBUTED BY WHITTAKER & WOODS

ABOVE: *In this child's room, the polka-dot* *headboard was painted to match the whimsic* *border, in which bears skate around the room* VILLAGE

ABOVE: *Good coordination creates a*
charming decor in this attic bedroom retreat.
The fabric colors match even though the prints
are different. SANDERSON

76

ABOVE: *A strong design, but beautifully implemented, in this large and interesting bath.*
GRAMERCY

LEFT: *A great example of a room in which fabrics and wallcoverings match in color but not in pattern. The exception is the window treatment, created from wallcovering-matched fabric.*
GRAMERCY

LEFT: *The gracefulness of this curved swag and floral border is a dynamic counterbalance to the linear striped pattern on either side of the bed.* VILLAGE

BELOW: *A linear look is emphasized by the wallcovering pattern, which complements the furnishings, floor mosaic, and glass panel adjoining the door.* IMPERIAL WALLCOVERINGS

FACING PAGE: *A straightforward woven pattern is a great starting point for a sparse, eclectic interior.* IMPERIAL WALLCOVERINGS

ABOVE AND FACING PAGE: *A retro 1950s look in this loft apartment benefits from a complementary background. The patterns in these two photos demonstrate how well the selections worked.* IMPERIAL WALLCOVERINGS

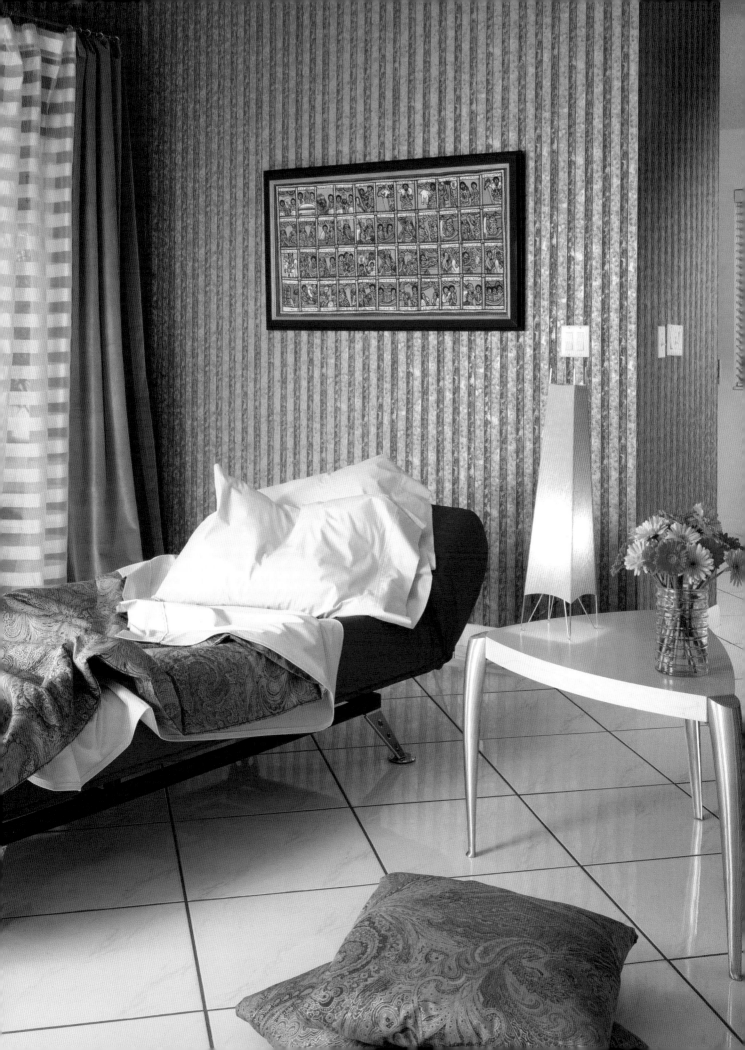

FACING PAGE: *A French country look has been achieved with this simple, yet elegant, striped wallpaper.* IMPERIAL WALLCOVERINGS

RIGHT: *This dining room gloriously combines the tropical with the traditional. The effect is paradoxical—a sort of relaxed grandeur.* GRAMERCY

BELOW: *A Fabergé egg collection print that is nothing less than stunning. By repeating the pattern in fabric details—the chair, ottoman, and pillow—the decorating efforts could be considered flawless.* GRAMERCY

LEFT: *An ingenious use of wallcovering and borders create an "alcove" in this country design.* DECORATING DEN INTERIORS

BELOW: *A painted pink ceiling softly offsets this lovely French country-style bedroom. The exquisite pattern on paper and fabric is a custom design.* BRUNSCHWIG & FILS

FACING PAGE: *A draped bed and matched fabrics, wallcoverings, and borders combine to create a room of sensationally coordinated style.* GRAMERCY

85

ABOVE: *A border defines this sweet, pleasantly coordinated nursery.*
DECORATING DEN INTERIORS

RIGHT: *The coordinating fabric to this wallcovering pattern was used for bedding.* SEABROOK WALLCOVERINGS

FACING PAGE: *This comfortable print, used throughout this small room, actually makes the room look larger than if different patterns were used.* BRUNSCHWIG & FILS

ABOVE: *Wallcovering may mimic a painted finish, as in this subtle selection that looks sponge-painted.* DECORATING DEN INTERIORS

RIGHT: *Softness is conveyed by this country-influenced room, from the upholstered screen to the sheer drapes. The starting point is the pale, light-on-light wallcovering.* GRAMERCY

FACING PAGE: *A distinctive border helps create the elegant ease of this room.* SCHUMACHER

LEFT: *A charming pattern for a charming room. This room in a mother-in-law's suite functions as a multipurpose room. What bette* *way to enjoy family activities than in this chee* *ful setting.* GRAMERCY

FACING PAGE: *An obvious choice for* *bathroom, and a fun one as well. The coor-* *dinating border in front of the base cabinet is* *nice touch.* SEABROOK WALLCOVERINGS

OVE: *This entryway encourages its occupants to be ever ready when it* *...es to a walkabout. The strong colors in the wide border print of mal-* *...ls, sunflowers, and pottery stand out against the more subdued striped* *...lcovering on the wall.* YORK WALLCOVERINGS

...GHT: *Theme-ing a room refers to repeating the dominant theme.* *...his case, a backdrop of tied flies used for fly fishing is picked up with the* *...der print and the decorative accessories in the room.* *...K WALLCOVERINGS*

...CING PAGE: *Vaulted ceilings are dramatic but this one is made* *...n more so with the use of a simulated cork ceiling. The effect makes the* *...m feel cozier.* YORK WALLCOVERINGS

Section 3

TEXTURE

TEXTURE GIVES THE ROOM ITS "FEEL." It comes into play in textiles, carpets, and wall finishes which can influence how you feel in a room and should be considered when you think about texture. All of your decorative treatments and objects in a room—even the amount of stuffing in the upholstery—add to the atmosphere of the room.

KNOW YOUR THREADS

This is a small sampling of the many textile options:

1. Voiles, organza, lace, and muslin are translucent fabrics appreciated for the bright, airy, modern elegance they lend to a room. When choosing a sheer fabric, pay attention to the care required: washable, natural fabrics are ideal.

2. Silks and damask are highly prized (cheaper versions are found in many fabric stores), and created on a jacquard loom to create a surface of matte and satin textures.

3. Velvets and tapestries are densely woven fabrics that lend an air of warmth, comfort, and drama.

4. Cottons, linens, and wools are organic fibers that are easily washed with little shrinkage. Cotton may be tightly or loosely woven, which will influence its strength and durability.

5. Acetate is a manufactured fabric that is convincing as artificial silk.

6. Viscose and rayon add strength to cottons and linens and adds sheen to highlight designs.

7. Chintz is a cotton that has been finished with a shiny glaze.

8. Brocade was originally made of silk, but is now produced with manufactured fibers.

Stone and metal will also contribute to a room's feel and texture. Aluminum, brass, steel, and wrought iron supply hardness and edge. Stone conveys a sense of weight and permanence and improves over time. Many types of stone may be used in furniture, flooring, and architectural accent.

Fabrics have long provided inspiration for home decorators, but they can also have a major environmental impact, softening hard surfaces and muffling sound.

When combined with trimmings, fabrics can complete a room.

For example, fringes and braids can accent, while cords and tassels can add movement and contrast.

The herringbone wood floor and antique rug highlight a medley of patterns and textures in this passageway. INTERIOR: DEUTSCH/PARKER DESIGN LTD.

Outfit your room for each season

The feeling of a room may be changed
during each season by thinking about
what textures are being emphasized.
For example, in the summer, a canvas
slipcover might can camouflage the
heavy brocade upholstery on the sofa,
or sisal can be laid over the carpeting
to create a lighter feeling underfoot.

Textures in stone

1. Marble looks as if it has frozen
   rivers running through it.
2. Slate has a rippled texture.
3. Limestone is smooth.
4. Granite is usually gray flecked
   with white but can also come in
   pink and beige.
5. Concrete is a common aggregate of
   stone that, when polished, can look
   sensational.

**Shape is an important trait to consider
when evaluating furniture. Round shapes,
as in this contemporary bedroom, are
thought to be more casual and warm,
where straight design is considered more
formal or restrained.** Interiors: Carrie
Brockman's Design Group

EVALUATE IMPORTANT SPACE AND COLOR CONSIDERATIONS

These questions will help you evaluate the space with which you have to work. They will also guide you through important considerations when choosing a color palette.

PHOTO: ERIC ROTH

1. Consider how you use the existing space in a room. Is there lots of open space? Does the furniture take up more than half the room?

2. What is the storage situation like? Could things be stored that are taking up space now?

3. Look for dead space, behind furniture, under cabinets. Could this space be used for storage? Could objects be rearranged to make it no longer dead space?

PHOTO COURTESY OF: CRATE & BARREL

4. There is enormous possibility in color choice for every room. Think about the colors themselves. What colors make you feel...

Invigorated?

_____

Relaxed?

_____

Cheerful?

_____

Calm?

_____

Friendly?

_____

5. Considering these emotions, which rooms would these colors be most appropriate for?

_____

_____

_____

INTERIOR DESIGN: PAMELA KARLYN MAZOW;
PHOTO: PETER JAQUITH

6. Think about who shares these rooms with you. Does your family have similar reactions to the colors as you?

_____

_____

_____

7. Consider the existing furniture and items that will be in the room. Are they compatible with the color of your choice? Do the patterns and the textures complement the palette?

_____

_____

_____

COLOR AND
TEXTURE

color and
texture

THE USE OF COLOR IN EASTERN CULTURES RANGES FROM THE JAPANESE AFFINITY FOR EARTHY, NEUTRAL TONES, OFTEN COMPLEMENTED WITH A BURST OF BOLD CLEAR PIGMENT, TO THE COMPLICATED INTERMINGLED HUES AND TONES FOUND IN PERSIAN CARPETS AND INDIAN BROCADES.

Ancient Eastern beliefs include much color symbolism that relates to the emotional responses the colors evoke. Modern-day science has corroborated what the ancients may have instinctively known. The Chinese five-color theory, a component of the practice of *Feng Shui*, associates a color with each of the five elements. Red, the color of fire, is considered auspicious. Science has determined that red invigorates and excites. Blue, the color of water, connotes spirituality. Blue soothes and cools. Green, the color of wood, indicates exuberant growth. It is uplifting and warm. Yellow, the color of earth, connotes wealth and power. Westerner's know it to be a color of contentment and harmony. White, the color of metal, is the color of fulfillment. White takes on different aspects depending upon its surrounding colors.

SILVER LEAF FURNITURE SETS AN OPULENT TONE. PAIR IT WITH SILKY FABRICS AND A WARM COLOR PALETTE FOR AN EXOTIC YET INVITING LOOK.

palette and
pattern

When you choose your colors, think of the responses they trigger. Keep in mind that combining colors introduces multiple attributes. Red can work in a bedroom, for example, if paired with a sufficient amount of a restful tone to quiet its effect.

     ✐ Add a bold splash of color to enliven a neutral palette. ✐ Use the Japanese tradition of monochromatic schemes and explore all values within a range. Add interest with pattern and texture. ✐ Evoke the mystique of India with brilliant colors in dazzling jewel tones.

     The Eastern affinity for natural fibers and materials introduces a broad range of textures. Woven natural fabrics, bamboo, lacquered wood, rice paper lanterns, sea grass carpets, linen, brocade, velvet, and raw silk all lend themselves to the East-West style.

     A variety of textures adds dimension to a monochromatic scheme. A sleek silk shantung pillow sham may be all that's needed to enliven a bedroom done in a single color. A crinkly unbleached cotton duvet cover can turn a stark bedroom into an inviting, cozy nook. With a palette of bold colors, let texture quiet the effect. Soft velvets or the rough texture of sea grass can tone down a vibrant hue.

     Don't ignore the textural effect of woods and porcelains. A shiny lacquered wood chest has a more enlivening effect than a rough, rustic one. A porcelain vase will gleam in a corner where an earthenware jug would quietly anchor the spot.

     Where complementary bold colors are used, match textures and patterns so the difference in the colors is the focal point. Where colors are similar or alike, vary textures wildly—a matelassé coverlet with embroidered, silky pillows, lacy white shams on a linen spread, sheer drapery against a concrete wall.

Photo: Paul Ferrino / Design: Peter Forbes

(above) USE COLOR AND TEXTURE TO SUBTLY UNIFY SEPARATE FUNCTIONAL AREAS OF AN OPEN FLOOR PLAN. THE ROYAL BLUE DINING ROOM CHAIRS ARE ECHOED IN THROW PILLOWS ON THE LIVING AREA SOFA. THE DARK EARTHEN TABLEWARE IS AKIN TO THE STONE FIREPLACE BEYOND.

(right) CHOOSE A GARDEN GATE OF WOOD SLATS AND STAINLESS STEEL TO ACT AS AN INTERESTING INTRODUCTION TO AN EAST-WEST HOME. THE SIMPLICITY OF LINE AND STRIKING JUXTAPOSITION OF MATERIALS MAKES A POWERFUL STATEMENT.

Photo: Luis Ferreira Alves / Architecture: Eduardo Souto Moura

CAPTURE THE EASTERN FEEL WITH A BOLD COLOR
SPLASH IN A NEUTRAL ROOM. SCULPTURAL
FURNISHINGS IN RICH ORANGE TONES SEEM TO FLOAT
IN A ROOM WITH UNADORNED WHITE WALLS AND
WINDOW TREATMENT. THE ROOM RADIATES AN
INVITATION TO SIT A WHILE.

Photo: Bjorg Arnarsdottir / Architect: Kar Ho Architect

(above) UPHOLSTER A CHAISE IN PEARLY GRAY SILK SHANTUNG BORDERED IN
SILK CORDING AND ACCENTED WITH TASSELS FOR A LOOK OF COOL
SOPHISTICATION. AN ASIAN LACQUERED CHEST AND SLEEK HARDWOOD
FLOORING MATCH THE SHEEN AND ADD DENSITY. SOFTEN THE EFFECT BY
FILTERING DAYLIGHT THROUGH BAMBOO SHADES.

(opposite) LAYER WHITE ON WHITE IN EMBROIDERED FLORAL MOTIFS AND
NUBBY RIBBING TO ADD DEPTH TO A PRISTINE BEDROOM. NATURAL LIGHT
FILTERED THROUGH TRANSLUCENT SHOJI-LIKE SCREENS AND WOODEN SLATTED
BLINDS GIVES THE ROOM A WARM GLOW.

Photo: Peter Margonelli / Interior Design: Benjamin Noriega-Ortiz

(above) USE BOLD COLORS FOR WALLS AS A BACKDROP FOR MINIMAL
APPOINTMENTS. HERE THE ELEGANT ORCHID DISPLAYED ON A GLASS-TOPPED TABLE
IS ALL THE ADORNMENT NECESSARY FOR THIS COLORFUL APARTMENT PALETTE.
EVEN WITH BOLD COLORS, SERENITY PREVAILS.

(right) TRANSFORM A SMALL BEDROOM INTO A REGAL EASTERN DELIGHT WITH
STRONG COLORS AND RICH FABRICS. SAFFRON, THE COLOR OF MONKS' ROBES,
PAIRED WITH MOST AUSPICIOUS DEEP RED CALLS FOR LUSTROUS BROCADES AND
SILKS. HIGHLY POLISHED WOOD FURNISHINGS AND CANDLELIGHT COMPLETE THE
OPULENT LOOK.

Photo and Design: Charlotte Jensen

(above) PAINT WALLS A DEEP, RICH RED FOR AN INSTANT EASTERN EFFECT.
BLACK LACQUERED FURNISHINGS ECHO THE SHEEN OF THE SATIN FINISHED
WALLS WHILE TRANSLUCENT SHOJI SCREENS KEEP THE GLOW FROM
OVERWHELMING.

(opposite) USE SLATE TILES FOR A RICH BACK SPLASH. TINY INLAID STONE
DETAIL ADDS A SUBTLE NOTE. GIVE THE RANGE HOOD A THIN COAT OF HONEY
COLORED PLASTER TO RELIEVE THE DARK PURPLISH-BLUE OF THE SLATE.
ABSTRACT DRAWINGS CUT INTO THE PLASTER AS IT DRIES TRANSFORMS AN
UTILITARIAN SURFACE INTO ART. THE ROUGH NATURAL SURFACES ARE GIVEN
ADDED LIFE AS THEY GLINT OFF THE STAINLESS STEEL COUNTERTOP.

113

Photo: Peter Margonelli / Interior Design: Benjamin Noriega-Ortiz

Photo: Dorothy Perry / Design: Tangee Harris-Prichett

(above) IN A SITTING AREA WITH AN ECLECTIC MIX OF FURNISHINGS, PROVIDE COHESION THROUGH COLOR AND TEXTURE. A BRIGHTLY COLORED WOOL RUG GROUNDS THE OTHERWISE NEUTRAL COLOR SCHEME, WHILE AN EAMES SOFA AND A NOGUCHI COFFEE TABLE PROVIDE SMOOTH LINES AND SLEEK SURFACES. THE WICKER CHAIRS AND SLATTED BLINDS GIVE THE ROOM AN AIRY LIGHT-FILLED LOOK.

(left) HANG A BAMBOO SHADE AT THE HEAD OF A SIMPLE PLATFORM BED FOR DEFINITION AND AS A VISUAL LINK TO TATAMI MATS USED AS CARPETING. TRY LUSH ULTRASUEDE BEDCOVERS IN RICH OCHRE AS A TEXTURAL COUNTERPOINT. SHOJI SCREENS LIGHTEN AND RELIEVE THE MONOCHROMATIC COLOR SCHEME.

(opposite) CHOOSE WARM EARTH TONES FOR A SENSUOUS BEDROOM. PAIR THE ROUGH TEXTURES OF WOOD AND LEATHER NATIVE AMERICAN ART WITH SOFTLY RIBBED CHENILLE ON A FUTON FOR EAST-WEST IMPACT AND TACTILE DELIGHT.

Photo: Tim Lee / Interior Design: Ho Sang Shin, Antine Associates

(opposite) USE CALMING JADE TONES FOR DOMINANT COLOR TO CREATE A RESTFUL BEDROOM. THE BED, A PLATFORM UPHOLSTERED IN JADE GREEN, IS DRESSED WITH BLANKETS AND PILLOWS IN NEUTRAL TONES. THE FLORAL PILLOWCASES AGAINST THE STRIPED SHAMS ADD INTEREST AND ARE GROUNDED BY THE TEXTURE OF THE BLANKET. BAMBOO SHADES CREATE AN AURA OF THE EAST. GREEN BORDERS FOR TOP SHEET AND ACCENT PILLOW CREATE UNITY OF COLOR WITHIN THIS TEXTURAL MEDLEY.

(above) USE ANALOGOUS COLORS IN SHIMMERING FABRICS. JUXTAPOSE GREEN AND ORANGE, LINKED BY THEIR SHARED YELLOW COMPONENT, FOR A BOLD COLOR STATEMENT. IDENTICAL FABRICS KEEP THE COLOR SCHEME FROM BECOMING OVERPOWERING. THE SILKY SHEEN AND STRAIGHTFORWARD PATTERN ADD STABILITY.

Photo: Alan Weintraub / Design: Barry Brukoff

(above) TAKE ADVANTAGE OF THE BEAUTY AND PRACTICALITY OF SLATE FLOOR TILES IN THE
ENTRYWAY. STIPPLE-PAINT WALLS IN A COPPERY TONE FOUND IN THE VARIEGATED SLATE TO
GIVE THE AREA A WELCOMING, EARTHY GLOW.

(opposite) COLOR AND TEXTURE ARE ALMOST INSEPARABLE IN VARIEGATED SLATE TILES.
ACCENTUATE THE RICH GOLDEN TONES WITH LIMESTONE FLOOR TILING AND PUNCTUATE
WITH A NATURAL CHERRY WASHSTAND. RAFFIA MATS SUBTLY ADD TO THE OUTDOOR APPEAL
OF THIS BATH.

Photo: Jeff McNamara / Design: Austin Patterson Disston

Photo: Ira Nowinski / Design: Levitt/Weaver

(opposite) ACHIEVE A TRANQUIL LOOK IN THE BATHROOM WITH THE MUTING EFFECT OF
UNPOLISHED STONE FOR COUNTERS AND TUB SURROUND. PAIRED WITH RUSTIC WOOD THE
LOOK IS SIMPLE AND NATURAL. WHITE PORCELAIN FIXTURES AND WHITE WALLS CONTRAST
WITH THE DARK ELEMENTS AND GIVE THE ROOM ITS CLEAN, FRESH FEELING.

(above) FACE A SHOWER WALL WITH CAST ROCK TO CAPTURE THE ESSENCE OF BATHING IN A
MOUNTAIN STREAM. AWASH IN NATURAL LIGHT, THE TEXTURED SURFACE TAKES ON ADDED
DEPTH AND GIVES THE ROOM A FRESH AIR FEELING. A CONCRETE TUB SURROUND
COMPLEMENTS THE WALL TREATMENT AND ADDS TO THE AURA.

Photo: Steve Vierra Photography / Design: Anthony Catalfano

(left) GIVE YOUR ROOM POSITIVE ENERGY, WARMTH, AND VITALITY WITH BOLD RED. HERE UPHOLSTERY FABRIC REMINISCENT OF CHINESE PEONIES CALMS THE RED WITH ITS GOLD BACKGROUND.

(opposite above) CHOOSE BAMBOO FURNISHINGS TO TONE DOWN THE AUSTERITY OF DARK BEAMS. INTRODUCE THE TEXTURES OF RAW SILK AND TAPESTRY FOR A RICH MIXTURE IN NATURAL TONES.

(opposite bottom) CREATE AN ETHEREAL SLEEPING SPACE WITH A CANOPY BED CARVED IN AN EASTERN STYLE. A BOLD BUT RESTFUL SILK-SCREENED RED BEDCOVER BALANCES A GOSSAMER DRAPERY FOR THE PERFECT BLEND OF AIRY AND GROUNDED. THE OUTDOOR FEEL OF THIS SLEEPING PORCH CAN BE DUPLICATED INDOORS WITH TEXTURAL NATURAL WINDOW TREATMENTS AND POTTED GREENERY.

Photo: Jaime Ardiles-Arce / Design: Sandra Nunnerly

(opposite) USE SAFFRON GOLD TO INFUSE A REGAL EASTERN NOTE. THIS EXOTIC PRINT INTRODUCES A COMPLEMENTARY VIOLET TONE AND GIVES UPHOLSTERED BANQUE SEATING AN ELEGANT AIR.

(above) USE RED, THE MOST AUSPICIOUS COLOR ACCORDING TO ANCIENT CHINESE WISDOM, FOR A ROOM THAT INSTANTLY EXCITES AND ENLIVENS. A DEEP TONE IN SATIN FINISH BECOMES AN ELEGANT BACKDROP WITH AN EASTERN FEEL.

SOFTEN THE ROUGH-HEWN TEXTURES OF ARCHITECTURAL ELEMENTS WITH NATURAL COTTON BEDDING AND GOSSAMER WHITE DRAPERY FOR AN APPEALING BEDROOM. TRANSLUCENT SLIDING CLOSET DOORS INTRODUCE FILTERED LIGHT AND DESIGN APPEAL WHILE SERVING TO CONCEAL CLOSET CLUTTER.

Photo: David Glomb / Design: Insight West (Goers and Williamson)

Photo: Jacques Dirand / Design: Christian Liaigre

128

Photo: Jacques Dirand / Design: Christian Liaigre

(opposite) PROVIDE RELIEF FROM SOLID, FINISHED WOOD SURFACES IN A BEDROOM WITH

RATTAN HEADBOARDS, COMPLEMENTED WITH CORDED STRAW ARMCHAIRS THAT ADD A SUBTLE

TEXTURAL TWIST OF THEIR OWN. IMAGINE HOW DIFFERENT THIS ROOM WOULD FEEL WITH

POLISHED WOOD HEADBOARDS AND UPHOLSTERED CHAIRS.

(above) GIVE A CASUAL COUNTRY LIVING ROOM EAST-WEST APPEAL WITH SURPRISING

TEXTURAL JUXTAPOSITIONS. LUSH VELVET AND EBONIZED WOOD SOFTEN THE BACKDROP OF

WHITE WOOD-PANELED WALLS AND HARDWOOD FLOORING. A WOVEN AREA RUG UNDERFOOT

LINKS THE SEATING ELEMENTS AND WARMS THE ROOM.

Section 4

LIGHTING

YOU WILL WANT TO SEE YOUR HOME in the best light. Literally. Light affects mood, and how you light each room—whether with natural, artificial or candlelight—will influence how you feel about being there.

SEEING THE DIFFERENCE IN LIGHT

1. Natural: Provided through windows or portals, it provides the most soothing light. Its tone and intensity changes throughout the day and the year, and this ever-changing quality is part of natural light's charm. Study the flow of natural light through your home to make sure you use rooms and organize your tasks to take best advantage of this natural light. And remember: Colors look different under natural light than under artificial light.

2. Artificial: Artificial light is often necessary for a room to function properly so do not be afraid to equip your rooms with the needed amount of artificial lighting. There are many ways to introduce artificial light, including:

   a. Task lighting: Designed to illuminate specific activities, such as reading or cooking. It can be provided by halogen spotlights, desk lamps, floor lights, or shaded fluorescent strips.

   b. Accent lighting: Uses spotlights, picture lights, or strips in alcoves to pick out or enhance an interesting feature or item in a room.

   c. Decorative lighting: Try to blend candelabras or chandeliers into the style and color of the room. Uplights, also known as torchieres, add an extra dimension to a room at night, casting nice shadows as well as light onto walls and ceiling.

   d. Candlelight: Candles or oil lamps can introduce a soft, romantic, calming atmosphere to a space. Less powerful than an electric light, candles have a more dramatic effect.

If you need inspiration when planning your lighting, study how the professionals do it in showroom settings or how scenes are lit during a movie to create certain moods.

You will begin to discover that lighting is one of the decorator's handy tools to create a sense of architectural drama and surprise.

Candlelight is soothing and creates immediate atmosphere in a room. INTERIOR: MEADOWBANK DESIGNS INC.

Lighting may be used to accent certain features and to create dramatic "hot spots" in a room. Interior Design: Est Est, Inc.; Photo: Mark Boisclair

PHOTOGRAPHY | BRADY ARCHITECTURAL PHOTOGRAPHY | DESIGN | DIANE HARSCH

Illuminated glass, however small in area, expands space and suggests rooms beyond what is visible. Here, built-in glass shelves float a delicate display area and extend a small, U-shaped kitchen. The creative blend of ribbed glass and dark backsplash in a simple design adds to the illusion of depth.

Mirror is an unbeatable interior finish material that creates an illusion of space. Used with skill, mirrors can go almost unnoticed—while the atmosphere they create is appreciated. Exercise care to avoid reflecting ugly joints, utilitarian shelf brackets or unexpected revelations from neighboring areas.

Mirror can have backing of plain silver, bronze, antique finish, or smoke. Applications include the front of cabinetry; between counter surfaces and upper cabinets; wall to wall in bathrooms; or on a closet door. The doors in a narrow passage and the interior surfaces of bookcases can be sheathed in mirror to increase the illusion of space. Masking structural columns, chases for heating and plumbing, or other undesirable architectural features with mirror will not remove them from a room but will certainly make them less noticeable.

The same principle is true of artificial lighting; in confined spaces, the magic of artificial light creates the illusion of dimension and makes the actual floor area appear larger. Layering light in a room delivers depth to the space. Combining a floor uplight (hidden behind a plant), an overhead ceiling fixture, and a halogen reading lamp will paint the room with ambient light, accent and mood light, and task-oriented light. Mirrors and light are a melody and rhythm that can play in any room, regardless of size, and expand the dimension of a place without moving any walls.

expanding space
WITH MIRRORS AND LIGHT

Mirrors can serve as artwork while at the same time opening up a room. Choose a heavy, carved frame for emphasis, and determine the best size for the wall.

PHOTOGRAPHY
ERIC A. ROTH
DESIGN
GREGG CANN

Add light by perforating a wall with windows. This room presents a lovely rhythm of daylight that expands the space, with mirrors used in both traditional and whimsical ways. Try propping up a mirror any place that begs for sparkle.

PHOTOGRAPHY
ERIC A. ROTH
DESIGN
GREG CANN

This room is a sleek example of the use of mirrors and lighting to expand an area. Include incandescent uplights above cabinets for depth, or try low-voltage strip lights in the kick base of cabinets.

PHOTOGRAPHY | **BRADY ARCHITECTURAL PHOTOGRAPHY** | DESIGN | **DIANE HARSCH**

Shoji screens transform light into a luminous glow. You can use this concept of diffuse light in narrow space; work with sand-blasted glass, semi-opaque fabrics, or shoji-like plastic material from Japan.

PHOTOGRAPHY
CHARLOTTE JENSEN, ASID
DESIGN
CHARLOTTE JENSEN, ASID

Lighting adds sparkle to the stunning color and art in this 1,000-square-foot (93-square-meter) condo. The view from inside a tiny galley kitchen is dramatic and gallery-like.

PHOTOGRAPHY/DESIGN
CHARLOTTE JENSEN, ASID

Sculpture and art appear to pop away from the wall when lit properly from above, changing the dynamics of a small space. Try giving your artwork a dark background, and provide low-voltage halogen bulbs for the best and most intense light. Adjustable fixture heads allow for proper positioning of the light beam.

PHOTOGRAPHY/DESIGN
CHARLOTTE JENSEN, ASID

These windows pierce solid walls, allowing the room to "stretch." You can add windows with muntins, single lights, or specialty glass inserts.

PHOTOGRAPHY
SAM GRAY PHOTOGRAPHY
DESIGN
BIERLY-DRAKE

Light the face of a fireplace from above to add dimension. Create a focal wall by using recessed lights—position them two to three feet from the wall you want to accent.

PHOTOGRAPHY
ED GOHLICH
DESIGN
MARYCLARE BRANDT

This room demonstrates another successful union of windows, glass, and artificial lighting to build transparency and expand a confined dining area.

PHOTOGRAPHY
CAROL PEERCE
DESIGN
MARSHA SEWELL, ASID

Limited space means limited surface area for displaying art. These shallow niches offer the light a windowed wall would, with space to arrange valuable collections. Focal lighting can be added for dramatic emphasis, transforming each aperture into sculptural space. Together, these diminutive openings form a strong, luminous whole.

PHOTOGRAPHY
MARY E. NICHOLS
DESIGN
CHARLOTTE JENSEN, ASID

Here, a tiny dressing table hugs a flush mirror installation, and suddenly the bathroom expands. Consider a clean installation from the countertop to the ceiling for maximum effect.

PHOTOGRAPHY
STEVE VIERRA PHOTOGRAPHY
DESIGN
BEV RIVKIND

Install mirror under the cabinets to make a small bar area feel larger.

PHOTOGRAPHY
STEVE VIERRA PHOTOGRAPHY
DESIGN
SUSAN LEFKOWITZ

A mirrored wall offers an unobstructed view to the rest of the living area and patio windows beyond. A custom glass poker table enhances the light, airy feeling.

PHOTOGRAPHY
BRADY ARCHITECTURAL PHOTOGRAPHY
DESIGN
LAURA BIRNS, ASID

Cleverly placed sconce lights can make a simple archway a grand design element. This lighting plan also has the benefit of drawing attention upward, making the space seem dramatically larger.

PHOTOGRAPHY
COLL PHOTOGRAPHY
DESIGN
DOREE FRIEDMAN

The entrance of an apartment or townhouse that has no formal foyer can feel rather abrupt. Try covering a wall in the entry with a mirror. In this case, it serves as a background for a gracious console table.

PHOTOGRAPHY
BRADY ARCHITECTURAL PHOTOGRAPHY
DESIGN
KATHLEEN ZBACNIK, ASID

Creative and geometric,
a stepped mirror application on
a lavatory wall wonderfully reflects
the texture of silk wall covering
and colorful art and seems to
double the size of the room.

PHOTOGRAPHY
BRADY ARCHITECTURAL PHOTOGRAPHY
DESIGN
ANJUM RAZVI, ASID
BRENDA LANZA, ASID

Paired with mirror work, a wrap-around counter offers space for displaying decorative pieces as well as for functional items such as towels.

PHOTOGRAPHY
KIM BRUN PHOTOGRAPHY
DESIGN
CHRISTINE BRUN ABDELNOUR

built-in

FEATURES

When you design a cramped area, inches count; precision and ingenuity are your tools. The riddle of clever space utilization can be answered by using built-in features. First, analyze what the space should accomplish. Do you want to store or hide something? Do you require it to serve a double function? Is it for a private purpose, such as sleeping and grooming, or a more public one, like dining? Second, compile an inventory of the specific items to be accommodated: books, computer equipment, hobby supplies, CD player, television, appliances. Always have the complete dimensions readily available. Third, clear your mind of preconceived notions about room use, and make way for flexible thinking.

A typical 2-foot-by-6-foot (61 by 183 cm) closet in a guest bedroom can be transformed into a dresser or become a closet and kitchenette for a guest, concealed behind attractive bi-fold doors. An illusion of foreshortening occurs when the last 30 inches (76 cm) of a long, narrow room gain sleek shelves for a television and CD player with mirrored closet doors. The space above a sink becomes a floating display for delicate glass pieces with the addition of wall-to-wall glass shelves. Artful management of building materials transforms square walls into angles and shapes that roll out, pull apart, or slide up and down. Beds drop out of upholstered cupboards. Storage drawers hide beneath beds, and file drawers disguise themselves behind colorful panels.

Use materials appropriate to the character and style of your home to blend and conceal double functions. The prescription for success with a built-in unit includes proper scale, uninterrupted lines and connected elements, and careful planning.

PHOTOGRAPHY | **JEFF McNAMARA** | DESIGN | **AUSTIN PATTERSON DISSTON**

A built-in cupboard can have lots of personality. Here, the designer cut slats in the front panels to give them a lighter look and backed them with textured fabrics. You can add color or patterns, too.

Consider a recessed niche for a
built-in buffet. Here, it delivers a
perfect spot to showcase art in a
tiny breakfast nook.

PHOTOGRAPHY
MARY E. NICHOLS
DESIGN
CHARLOTTE JENSEN, ASID

Make your guests feel completely at home with a built-in dresser, hanging storage, and a place for luggage that can be closed off from the rest of a second bedroom. When you don't have guests, you can use the room as a spacious retreat, one uncluttered by a dresser and luggage rack.

PHOTOGRAPHY
BRADY ARCHITECTURAL PHOTOGRAPHY
DESIGN
KATHLEEN M. ZBACNIK, ASID

Recess a flexible file system into the wall, as seen on the left side of this narrow room. Include as many shallow shelves as possible for maximum storage in a home office.

PHOTOGRAPHY | BRADY ARCHITECTURAL PHOTOGRAPHY | DESIGN | LINDA MEDINA, ASID, AND MARYLIN MATSON

Apartment dwellers can also reap the benefits of custom built-ins. Add color to walls while taking advantage of the ingenuity of European wall systems, and take it with you when you move. Hang open or closed shelves, bookcases, glass shelves, and cabinets.

PHOTOGRAPHY
POLIFORM

A small living room usually means one wall for T.V., CD player, books, and display. You can make an artful arrangement that imitates custom built-ins by utilizing a wall-hung furniture system. Focus the center of the furniture arrangement on the dominant storage unit.

PHOTOGRAPHY
POLIFORM

The bottom of a built-in unit can provide hidden storage for games, photographs, and paperwork. Show off your favorite collection on its upper shelves; the display can change with your moods.

PHOTOGRAPHY
ERIC A. ROTH
DESIGN
KEN KELLEHER

A classic window seat offers
additional seating in a cramped
kitchen or dining room.

PHOTOGRAPHY
ERIC A. ROTH

PHOTOGRAPHY | ERIC A. ROTH | DESIGN | RICHARD EUSTICE

Bring bookshelves right to the edge of windows, and cover every inch of available wall space. Here, a library corner provides an inviting backdrop.

Design book nooks into the
architecture, as done here.
Anticipate your needs while
building, and you can integrate
this kind of feature seamlessly.

PHOTOGRAPHY
BRADY ARCHITECTURAL PHOTOGRAPHY
DESIGN
KATHLEEN M. ZBACNIK, ASID

Two types of built-in solutions are showcased here: an art niche pierced through a thickened wall and recessed wood shelves over flush lower cabinet doors. Remember to add downward-pointing lights to achieve dimension and create a useful display area.

PHOTOGRAPHY
COLL PHOTOGRAPHY
DESIGN
DOREE FRIEDMAN

Paired with Windsor chairs and
an old farm table, this built-in
kitchen seating creates a cozy,
family-oriented space for meals.

PHOTOGRAPHY
STEVE VIERRA PHOTOGRAPHY
DESIGN
SOIKELI + COMPANY

(right) Analyze your shelving use,
and make it as adaptable as possible. You can gain flexibility by
making shelves totally adjustable,
as in this well-designed pantry.

PHOTOGRAPHY
JEFF McNAMARA
DESIGN
AUSTIN PATTERSON DISSTON

Tuck a display shelf over a door. Don't forget about these opportunities to sneak in shelves. With them, you can create delightful visual surprises in your home.

PHOTOGRAPHY
COLL PHOTOGRAPHY
DESIGN
DOREE FRIEDMAN

Put a high display shelf in the
tiniest of bedrooms. You can
arrange stuffed animals, college
memorabilia, or decorative photo
boxes on it.

PHOTOGRAPHY
ERIC A. ROTH
DESIGN
DAWN SOUTHWORTH + DANA SALVO

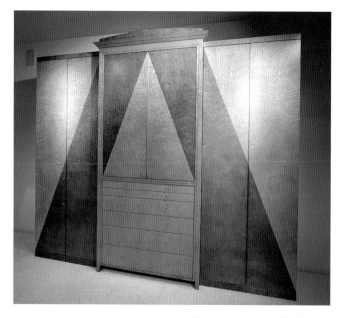

Custom design may offer the best built-in solution to your space crunch. Here, a custom armoire in three parts can be moved around to fit different space requirements.

PHOTOGRAPHY
KIM BRUN STUDIOS
DESIGN
CAROL G. BROWN, ASID

Unify space by blending built-in
features with architectural details.
Here, the doors and moldings
have the same stain as the custom shelving and cabinetry.

PHOTOGRAPHY
STEVE VIERRA PHOTOGRAPHY
DESIGN
ANN LENOX

Built-in features are wonderful for increasing efficiency in a small kitchen. Here, a stove hood doubles as storage and functional condiment ledge.

PHOTOGRAPHY
JEFF McNAMARA
DESIGN
AUSTIN PATTERSON DISSTON

Create a sleeping alcove with practical shelves tucked under a mattress.

PHOTOGRAPHY
STEVE VIERRA PHOTOGRAPHY
DESIGN
MIRIAN GLASGOW

PHOTOGRAPHY | ERIC A. ROTH | DESIGN | LLOY HACK ASSOCIATES

Keep built-in features in proportion to your room, as seen here in the low cubby-holes created for ceramics and books.

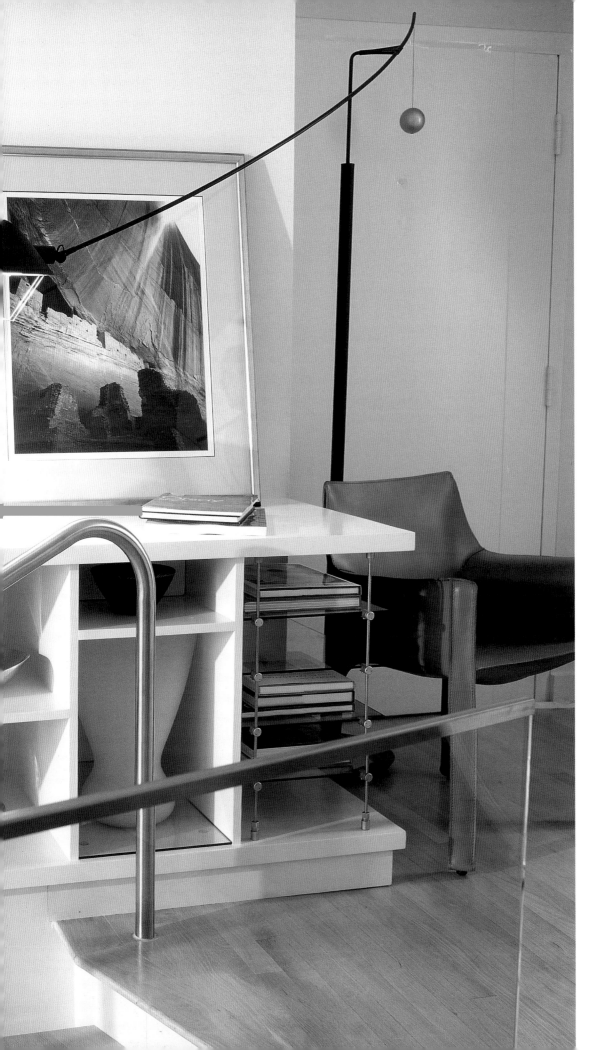

Section 5

FURNITURE AND FURNISHINGS

IF THE FLOOR AND THE WALLS ARE THE BODY OF A ROOM, THE FURNISHINGS ARE THE SOUL. Furniture is expressive and will help define the character of your home. Furniture also serves the most important function of home—your comfort.

Your attitude about furniture and furnishings for your home should be one of personal expression. At this stage of your decorating plan, you are translating the ideas that have moved you into rooms that will please you. But how should you make confident choices from the unending range of furniture available?

Before working up a new look, first look at the furniture and furnishings you already have. Can existing pieces be adapted with fresh paint or new upholstery? If you have a special item you want to keep in a particular room, use it as a starting point in establishing a decorative scheme.

When choosing new pieces, allow yourself time to assimilate them slowly enough so you can see how they work in your life. Consider their style and shape. Some people prefer furniture with lots of rounded edges, which feels more relaxed and informal. Others like furniture with straight lines, which looks and feels formal.

Foremost in your furniture decisions should be function and quality. Something that looks good will be dissatisfying if it is not useful or well made. Take your time in investing in the objects you want to live with. And on the larger items—beds, sofas and chairs—make sure they "feel" as wonderful as they look. Don't be afraid to flop into a chair or lie on a bed BEFORE you take it home.

The price of upholstery varies according to quality, but ideally an upholstered piece should last a lifetime with only the need for replacing the fabric. Choose a hardwood frame that is joined with screws, dowels and glue as opposed to glue alone. The best construction on upholstered items is called "eight-way," which means that each spring is attached by hand with knotted twine to the eight surrounding springs and to the webbing beneath. This attention to detail is costlier but your furniture will be more comfortable and durable.

Furniture styling: You already know what kinds of furniture you like.

Rather than seeking uniformity throughout your house, select the pieces based on the room.

A mish-mash of styles transforms a showplace into a comfortable home.

In this living room, cheerful furnishings create an aura of casual elegance while providing a comfortable and functional space. The fireplace suggests the natural placement for the grouping. INTERIOR DESIGN: DIANE WENDELL INTERIOR DESIGN

The feng shui way

Feng shui, the Chinese art of placement, has become a popular decorating tool. It follows a series of steps that include ridding yourself of physical and emotional clutter, drawing up a plan (begua), which is divided into nine sections that represent your life. By placing the begua over a plan of your home, the practitioner can suggest places to put objects to harmonize you, your items, and your home.

Weight is also a fairly accurate measure of quality. Pieces that "feel" heavier probably are made from hardwood rather than fabricated boards. If you can feel the back rail or if your legs bang against the wooden front edge, don't buy the piece.

Casegoods are pieces, usually wooden, that serve as containers, such as chests of drawers. Hardwoods such as mahogany will produce a longer-lasting casegood than softer woods such as pine.

WHAT'S YOUR TYPE?

The vocabulary for styles is relatively broad and there is a lot of cross-over. But a few of the broader categories include:

1. Americana: This is the look of paneled walls, grandfather clocks, brass candlesticks, Windsor chairs, and Persian rugs.
2. Fine Traditional: This look is influenced heavily by European accents such as ancestor portraits, Empire style furniture, heavy draperies, and silks, satins and brocades.
3. Contemporary: This is a futuristic styling with few curvy lines and much glass, steel, recessed lighting and monochromatic colors.
4. Country: This is look has a generous use of prints and large-scale floral patterns accented with basketry, folk art and subtle, weathered colors.

FURNITURE PLACEMENT

First establish the room's focal point. It can be a furnishing, a fixture, a view from a window, or a fireplace. When you have established each object in relationship to the focal point, you will want to relate it to the other objects as well.

Place your furniture according to where it makes the most economical and creative use of space. Room size and shape will inform the arrangement of furniture, at least of the larger pieces. But be willing to experiment. For example, do not automatically exclude large pieces from tiny spaces. An oversized piece can be a good focal point in a small room.

In placing your furniture, try to have a balance of items in every room—some decorative, some practical, some purely fun. Ultimately the furniture should be arranged to reflect the needs of the people who use it, but resist the need to cram everything into one room.

Furniture can also be placed strategically to create "zones" for different activities. For example, if you have a television in the room, don't arrange the seating in such a way that everyone is forced to watch it. By placing the television in a corner rather than in front of the sofa, you can arrange the remaining furniture in such a way that it creates a quiet zone for conversation or reading.

Raffia mats are stacked and topped with glass to make a casual end table.

INTERIOR DESIGN: BRIAN MURPHY; PHOTO: TIM STREET-PORTER

Crafty camouflage

Slipcovers, available ready-made or custom, are a stylish, practical way of dressing furniture. They can be used to disguise worn pieces, add visual flair, change the look with the seasons, or just extend the life of the fabric beneath. Slipcovers can be used on sofas, chairs, and chaises and are best when kept simple with piping or bound seams.

"Furnishings" are what designers call the pillows, tiebacks, vases, and objects in a room. Someone else might call them knickknacks, but furnishings suggests that the items have meaning, whereas knickknacks suggests disposable objects.

The arrangement of furnishings has much to do with detail. In planning a room, it is easy to focus only on the main elements—walls, windows, etc. Yet the little touches make rooms bloom. Books, aquariums, artwork, and flowers add the flourish and layers.

In the decorative sense, every accessory—a pitcher, a vase, a tablecloth—is a chance to introduce color and spirit to a room. However, it also becomes one more presence in the room competing with other objects, so you might think about which objects to display and which to store.

Restraint is the key to elegant rooms where each item is allowed space to display its virtues. The more objects, the more space they will seem to occupy— but the cozier the room might feel to some.

Choose pieces of furniture that are the right size for tiny areas. Here, a table is nestled in front of a fireplace, enabling traffic to get around it.

Be suspicious of step-by-step formulas for furniture arrangements. Look at your raw space and evaluate its architectural features, constraints, and peculiarities. You don't need an expert to tell you about the height of your ceilings, your limited wall space, or the location of the fireplace. You know better than anyone the traffic patterns of your home and how you would like to use each room. In small rooms, the most important characteristics of furniture are size and dimension. Interior designers use "in scale" and "out of scale" to describe pieces as acceptable or totally wrong for a particular space. Getting the size, look, and placement just right takes thought and keen observation.

If your room is limited in actual floor area but blessed with high ceilings, you might try larger sizes of furniture. Consider using relatively strong colors on walls if your room features large windows or French doors. But when your room has little natural light, take care to keep the feel of furnishings simple and delicate rather than substantial. There are times when a tiny room can charm with the sensation of overstuffed comfort, and other times when sleek simplicity is the solution. Balance furniture arrangements with symmetrically placed objects—two chairs opposite one sofa, for instance, or a heavy, bulky object countered by one that has strong, bold color. Art on a wall above a piece of furniture can provide needed balance or a shout of counterpoint that enlivens the atmosphere. Think about your purpose first and the position of furniture next. Try to be flexible; you may have to rid yourself of furniture that will not work, doesn't enhance your comfort or aesthetic experience, or blocks the successful use of an area.

furniture

A small-scale armchair is
accompanied by a small side
table. Make certain that the
arms of your furniture are not
eating up all the space. And
keep in mind that everything
does not have to match; in fact,
it's better if it doesn't. Free
yourself to use individual furniture pieces that are the right
style for the look.

PHOTOGRAPHY
CAROL PEERCE
DESIGN
MARSHA SEWELL, ASID

Even seemingly insignificant details like small display items or a well-placed sign can spice up a small room.

PHOTOGRAPHY
SAM GRAY PHOTOGRAPHY
DESIGN
BIERLY-DRAKE

An enclosed sun porch can become part of your interior space. This sitting area off the kitchen functions like a small family room. Once again, the ottoman appears as a coffee table.

PHOTOGRAPHY
JEFF McNAMARA
DESIGN
AUSTIN PATTERSON DISSTON

(right) A bay window is a wonderful place to display art without interfering with the flow of traffic in a room.

PHOTOGRAPHY
CAROL PEERCE
DESIGN
MARSHA SEWELL, ASID

Sometimes one well-chosen piece is all you need to complete a small space. In this case, it's a bench that has a lot of character. You can also try a narrow table or shallow cabinet.

PHOTOGRAPHY
COLL PHOTOGRAPHY
DESIGN
DOREE FRIEDMAN

This room combines honest symmetry with bold lines. The furniture is simple and architectural in feel but not out of scale with the space. Choose a few strong furniture pieces to communicate your look clearly.

PHOTOGRAPHY
POLIFORM

Antiques suit small, traditional rooms. Pieces like the bed seen here were originally designed with little floor space and high ceilings in mind. The scale in this bedroom is perfect.

PHOTOGRAPHY
ERIC A. ROTH
DESIGN
PETER WHEELER

Tiny does not equal boring. Here, a small bench is placed at one end of the dining table surrounded by armless chairs. Experiment with chair frames and fabrics that don't match for a tasty solution to furnishing a small dining room.

PHOTOGRAPHY | ERIC A. ROTH | DESIGN | PAT STAVARIDIS

Switch living and dining furniture, and dine in front of your fireplace. Instead of a sofa and chairs, four comfortable armchairs ring an upholstered ottoman coffee table. Try replacing bulky sofas with chairs; guests prefer their own personal space anyway.

Pull furniture away from the perimeter of your room and angle it to make it look more interesting. If the size of the pieces is correct, it will not matter that the room is small.

PHOTOGRAPHY
ERIC A. ROTH
DESIGN
DOMAIN HOME FURNISHINGS

Revisit the idea of symmetrical and traditional room arrangements, but break the old rules. Use furniture to break up a small room into separate, functional areas.

PHOTOGRAPHY
ERIC A. ROTH
DESIGN
MANUEL de SANTAREN, INC.

Antique shops are great places
to look for small-scale furniture
like the pieces pictured here.

PHOTOGRAPHY
ERIC A. ROTH
DESIGN
ROBERT MIKLOS

Place a simple oversize chair with floor cushions in front of a fireplace for a cozy effect. Try different types of floor pillows or low benches, which are unobtrusive, for a variety of casual seating arrangements.

PHOTOGRAPHY
JEFF McNAMARA
DESIGN
AUSTIN PATTERSON DISSTON

Convert everyday objects,
contemporary finds, or relics of
the past into unusual furnishings.
Rescued from a corner of an
attic, old-fashioned suitcases
make a charming coffee table
that brings even more personality
to this eclectic setting.

INTERIOR DESIGN: **PAUL MAGNUSSEN**

191

Hunt for an interesting bench, such as the one used here, to act as a very narrow coffee table. Benches are the perfect scale for a tight space and are easy to find.

PHOTOGRAPHY
ERIC A. ROTH
DESIGN
PETER WHEELER

Consider using an ottoman that can double as a coffee table. You'll want to select a durable fabric; this one's covered in raffia. Velvet and silk are gorgeous but not practical in this instance. Try leather, synthetic woven materials, and textures that disguise soiling.

PHOTOGRAPHY
SAM GRAY PHOTOGRAPHY
DESIGN
BIERLY-DRAKE

Attic rooms produce unusual challenges and space. This upstairs bedroom in a 450-square-foot (42-square-meter) cottage has just the right size furniture. Notice the delicacy in the vintage iron bed frame and petite side tables.

PHOTOGRAPHY
SAM GRAY PHOTOGRAPHY
DESIGN
BIERLY-DRAKE

If you light the space under a stairway properly, it can become a great spot for a home desk. This little work area is suited to writing correspondence and paying bills. An area like this could also be designed with custom built-ins for a computer workstation.

PHOTOGRAPHY
ERIC A. ROTH
DESIGN
PETER WHEELER

A simple side table can be
dressed with a table skirt and
double as a sideboard for a
dining area.

PHOTOGRAPHY
ERIC A. ROTH
DESIGN
PAT STAVARIDIS

Section 6

AMBIANCE

Harmony in a home
may be created by
unifying the rooms
with color.

For example,
painting a door in
the same shade as
the upper walls of the
adjoining room unites
the two spaces and
defines each area.

TO CREATE AN ATTRACTIVE AND COMFORTABLE SPACE is, in a sense, creating a harmony of the things that make you feel at home. The way the rooms look, feel, and smell are important; you do not want to live in a home that is jarring to you.

Think of your house or apartment as a series of spaces linked together. Remember that one room can be seen from another. By thinking of rooms in relation to the whole, you will be able to create environments and traffic patterns that don't jar.

All design issues involve noise control. What you can or cannot hear is important in creating a comfortable home. For inside noise, a home decorating center will have a variety of acoustical tiles that may be added as padding to walls, ceilings or floors, to create relatively sound-proof rooms. For outside noise from cars, construction and chattering, structural changes that include insulated walls and windows, floating floors and using heavy materials such as concrete and stone for walls of rooms of particular concern.

Smell has the power to trigger emotions and create a sense of well-being. First seek to improve the air quality in your home by circulating fresh air, even if you only open a window. To make the air more sensual and relaxing, you should begin to experiment with the many varieties of diffusers that introduce scents into the air. Scented candles, lamp rings, and potpourri burners are very popular and readily available. Sprays and plug-in air fresheners provide an economical means of introducing scent.

MEDITATION SPACE: CREATING A CALM PLACE

Your home needs to provide a place for your many moods, including the need to be apart from the rest of it. If there is a place that you can turn into a "quiet zone," you may find it reassuring. Houses need to accommodate a change of moods and at least one room in the house should be devoted to this. In modern design language, these spaces are increasingly called "meditation rooms."

Window seats provide great opportunity for building in quiet zones without much fuss. PHOTO: ROBERT PERRON

If there is room for space for quiet reflection, the decor should tend towards the austere. Solid, calm, subdued colors with no patterns have proven the most relaxing hues. Subtle and deep shades of blue, green, black, yellow or red are said to encourage concentration and analysis. The furnishings need be no more than a pile of pillows or a chaise lounge. Your lighting could be by candle. (Never introduce a clock.)

If it is impractical to devote a large space for quiet contemplation, then try to think of ways to incorporate quiet spots into your home. Old homes have many idiosyncratic spaces that may be easily converted in quiet zones. A window seat or alcove can become a magical space if treated as a pocket for peaceful minutes.

In every home there should be a connection with nature, with the outdoors, and for many, plants and flowers are the answer. They can add height, color, variety, camouflage and drama to a room. Plus, plants help the air quality in the room.

Flowers always freshen a room, and bouquets need not be fancy nor expensive. Choosing flowers of the same hue will pick up a dominant color in the decorations. As with any decorative element, increasing mass and volume elevates impact—remember that, depending on your mood, a single stem may have as much drama as dozens. Rooms look awkward when there is a mishmash of conflicting styles and tastes competing for attention.

Also important to consider in decorating a small space is scale. Resist the notion that a small room should be empty, because a small space with little in it will always remind you of its limited size, but one that is elegantly laid out and thoughtfully furnished to an appropriate scale has its own atmosphere and character.

Keep your decorating designs simple; don't allow the floor or window decorations to get out of control.

Gloss paint on the room's walls, ceilings, and floors will reflect light and lend the illusion of more space.

Select wallpapers with geometric patterns on a white or pale background that lend the illusion of depth to a small space. Vertical stripes, on wallpaper or painted, tend to make a room look "taller."

In small spaces, you will want to flood the walls with color and light to keep the space large.

Shades of off-whites in variegated textures are combined with teak and cane furnishings to create a sophisticated Anglo-Indian mood in this island retreat.

DESIGN: MICHAEL DE SANTIS

199

LIGHTING AND FURNITURE choices are essential for any room. These important questions will help you plan lighting and furniture.

PHOTO COURTESY OF BRUNSCHWIG & FILS

1. What kind of lighting do you have now? (Recessed, chandelier, floor lamps., etc.)? Is this form adaptive to change with little investment?

2. How would a change of lighting scheme improve the mood of the room?

3. Is the lighting functional and compatible with the activities performed in the room? A room for reading should have adjustable spot lighting; kitchens should have good overhead lights.

4. Would a fresh coat of paint liven up furniture that you are getting tired of?

5. Would a slipcover help carry it through another season?

_____

_____

_____

_____

6. Is all your furniture a certain style or does it vary by room or piece?

_____

_____

_____

_____

7. Is there some element that you could add to all of it to make it more cohesive?

_____

_____

_____

_____

INTERIOR DESIGN: AUSTIN PATTERSON DISSTON; PHOTO: JEFF MCNAMARA

PHOTO COURTESY OF: CRATE & BARREL

Chapter 3

DESIGN IN FIVE

Easy Pieces

THE ROOM IS LIKE A TREE with many branches that relate to the whole. Decorating a space will be more fruitful if you look at a room's five easy pieces: walls, floors, windows, ceilings, and passages. Each of these pieces is explored separately in this chapter.

In this living room, a soft yellow palette accented by black provides a neutral backdrop for the room's focal point. Ashwood and steel lamps and brushed steel sconces are textural accents. INTERIOR DESIGNER: LETELIER & ROCK DESIGN, INC.

WALLS

WHAT IS A WALL?

A wall is a partition between open space that may be temporary or permanent. When four walls enclose a space with an entryway, it now has "room."

A wall is really made up of many parts that have names in the vocabulary of architecture. The uppermost border on a wall is the cornice or crown molding—a projecting ornamental molding where the wall joins the ceiling.

For a long time, the cornice was considered essential if a room was to look "finished," but many homes built since the 1950s sometimes lack such detailed features. A crown molding can be added relatively easily. The cornice can be painted in various ways or the color of the ceiling can be continued down over it (this will render the cornice blend less distinguishable).

The area of the wall just below the cornice is known as the frieze. (If your walls lack this, borders can create the illusion of friezes.) Below the frieze the wall falls away to the skirting board (baseboard) at floor level. Sometimes, the wall has a chair rail and a dado (wainscoting) at waist height or higher.

Since walls constitute the largest surface areas in the room at eye level, the primary decisions involve whether and how to cover them. Color and pattern on walls may be added in many ways by paint, paper, or fibers.

PAINT ON WALLS

Paint is the easiest of the decorator's tools. Inexpensive and easily undone, it may be a good surface treatment for the beginning decorator. However, elaborate treatments may also be created with special painting techniques.

Color can be decoration enough, especially if the color is strong. When thinking about which color and patterns for your walls, consider what you'd really enjoy living with. Picking out a single, solid wall color requires much attention and thought about how the color and room's function will mesh.

Paint finish is also an important consideration. Three types of finish are readily available: a soft matte, eggshell (soft but with a slight sheen) and satin, the shiniest of the three.

Walls are said to stir our most primitive instincts.

Walls that are too close together make us feel confined.

Walls too far apart make use feel lost or small.

Where walls should go is half of your decorating plan—what walls should wear is the other.

Hand-painting stripes on walls is a whimsical touch in a formal entry foyer. Antique pink luster adds color. Interior Design: Elizabeth Read Weber, ASID, LLC

Walls painted a solid color function as a backdrop, setting off and complementing a room's decorative scheme. You could decorate a wall with a less intense, non-uniform finish by using various paint techniques such as stippling, ragging, sponging, or distressing. These decorative techniques of applying paint all diffuse the color without diluting the shade itself.

Colorwashing: This paint technique gives a "barely there" finish to walls. This dreamy, translucent effect is achieved by building up many layers of diluted paint to give a greater depth of color. It involves applying a thin glaze over a base coat with a brush or roller, or even a cloth or a sponge. The result is a gentle gradation of color that is less evenly distributed than in sponged effects.

Stamping and block printing: Rubber stamps and ink pads may have once been associated only with paper, but that's just the beginning for adventurous home decorators. A wall provides a wonderfully large palette for images applied with rubber stamped images onto a painted surface. Many sophisticated, stylish designs in rubber stamps are available, as are inks that are suitable for fabrics.

Simple designs give the best effects. A wall painted with emulsion is the ideal stamping surface. Surfaces that are matte and flat present less likelihood that the stamp will slide as you apply pressure. (A gloss surface is not ideal because the wet paint on the stamp will slide on a slick surface.)

PAPER ON WALLS

Wallpaper as a tool of interior decoration has a relatively recent history. Before Elizabethan times, most walls were adorned with tapestries or other textiles.

Commercial wallpapers in many designs are usually available through design and decorating centers. Most papers fall into one of three categories: non-washable; washable, which are usually plastic-coated surfaces that can be wiped clean with a damp sponge; and scrubbable, which are vinyl or vinyl-filled and can withstand scrubbing with non-abrasive cleansers (they work well in high-use areas such as children's rooms, kitchens, and baths).

Recycled paper in the form of maps, newspapers, book jackets, photocopies of your pet, and almost anything else that is paper and water-soluble is potential wallpaper. Test your paper source by using commercial wallpaper paste on a small test area of the wall you want to paper, and see what happens with the paper's color and texture before you proceed to a larger surface. With this type of collage treatment, you aren't after perfection of image, but rather the spirit of the wall's surface.

Movable Walls

Flexible walls can be created out of almost anything and placed anywhere. They include screens, curtains, room dividers—in short, anything that conceals part of a room without denying that that other space exists. Almost anything can become one: a bookcase turned sideways, or a high-back sofa positioned just so.

Dramatic fabrics make excellent wall coverings. Interior Design: Noha & Associates; Photo: Jon Miller, Hedrich Blessing

Testing Paint Colors

A paint chip is usually too small to indicate how paint will look on a wall. Designers suggest testing as large a swath as possible, up to three feet square—on the wall, or on a board propped against it. You should check the sample under day and evening lighting conditions.

Fool the eye

Dark or warm-colored walls, whether papered or painted, have a richer, more "finished look" than white or pale ones. Pale walls can be made to look more interesting with a border of paper or of grosgrain or velvet ribbon stuck on the wall with a glue-gun or a strong adhesive.

FIBERS ON WALLS

Fabric gives a rich surface to walls. When applied over an interlining, fabric can deaden sound and provide warmth to a room. Because of the obvious cleaning challenges, fabric should cover walls unlikely to be stained easily by water or grease.

Quilts, blankets and decorative rugs of all shapes and patterns can be used to add texture, warmth, color and visual excitement to walls. Because of their size, these textiles can also be used to cover up imperfections in your wall.

Textiles such as tapestries and wallhangings can also become decorative wall-coverings. Architectural screens of fabric also provide value as temporary walls to help divide space or provide privacy in multipurpose spaces.

Natural fibers such as woven raffia, sisal or coir matting backed with paper are among the least expensive of the natural coverings available for use on walls. Attached with staple guns, natural fibers on walls provide a nubby texture and neutral color that speaks of informality. Natural fibers in a refined finish can also be dressed up when paired with more sophisticated objects in the room.

TILES ON WALLS

Tiles made from fired clay or natural materials such as stone, slate or marble provide a finish and texture and lend an air of stability and permanence to a space.

Just as you would with paint, use the colors of tile to blend or contrast with other colors in a room. Depending on the color, pattern, and number of walls tiled, the room could be "heavy" or "fragile" in feeling if too much or too little wall surface is tiled. Consider tiles as accents or as treatment for one wall that is the focal point.

OTHER POSSIBILITIES

Metals are available in thin enough dimensions to be applied easily to wall surfaces. Sheets of mesh or metal "fabric" with metallic sheen may add luster to wall surfaces. These metal fabrics may be rough or smooth and can be applied as you would fabric or paper.

Sheet metal and aluminum sheets are chic but sometimes expensive. Stainless steel is even more of a luxury. Copper and brass are also available in sheets, but like all metals, they dull easily and need lots of polishing.

Glass blocks may be used to define a wall or to establish a space. Many varieties are available through home decorating centers.

Wood paneling in modern interiors can be practical and decorative. Because the surface of paneling is tough and can withstand knocks, paneling provides a practical advantage in service areas such as hallways, stairs and bathrooms.

For decorative use, half-paneling up to a dado level has always been a means to combining the advantages of a practical surface, on the parts of the wall that receive most wear—at kid- and kicking-level. Different styles of paneling now available provide some design interest. Consider the size of panels in relation to the scale of the room. For example, smaller panels generally work better in smaller rooms.

Hardwood paneling is usually not painted but left to display its beauty as naturally as possible; softwood paneling has always been painted. (Painting paneling might provide an interesting decor change but it is sometimes a difficult process to undo without scratching the paneling's surface.)

Fabric screens customized to be temporary walls in this living room provide dramatic visuals and the flexibility of being moveable. Interior Design: Jane J. Marsden Antiques & Interiors, Inc.

Using Borders

Borders give walls definition and a sense of importance. This detail conveys a sense that a wall is "finished." Wallpaper patterns will often have a border pattern for decorative contrast. But anything may become a border. Why not collect a bunch of beautiful shaped leaves and glue each one, end to end just under the cornice for a fresh, seasonal feeling, however short-lived?

OBJECTS ON WALLS

Walls are a natural place for display. A large painting on a wall will focus attention on it, so the first question about placement is whether you want this piece to be in the foreground or the background. Where you should to hang it will determine its importance in the room.

Ideally, photographs, paintings, and posters should be hung at eye level to encourage study. If a collection of images is not related, give the items a related look by using either a similar matting or framing.

Symmetry is a most reliable approach to arranging collections of images. Don't hang pictures too high or too far apart. Experiment with where you'd like to see things before you get out a hammer to hang anything. Rotating these hanging items will prevent visual boredom and revitalize a room.

Many wall-mounted fixtures, other than picture frames, can be used to mount or hold images and objects. Shelving, clips, and ceiling-mounted hangers allow much flexibility in displaying paintings, photographs, or posters. Even a clothesline draped across a room provides a wonderful place to display pictures and postcards.

SELECTING FRAMES

If your photo or painting is worth a thousand words, consider the value you place in its frame. Selecting the appropriate frame is as important as where you place the item.

Small frames focus the eye on detail, while medium and large frames help expand spaces by lending a sense of proportion and depth, particularly if you invest to have the image matted and mounted. Scour second-hand stores and flea markets to find old frames that can be used artfully in your home. You may even choose to make your own frames.

COLLECTIBLES

Bring out your collections and review them for possible use as wall decor. Almost any collection can be impressive when viewed as part of a thoughtful display. One way to think about displaying collectibles on walls is to consider how you want the object to appear. For example, placing objects on glass and lighting them from beneath lends a museum quality to the display.

Picture Hangers

When photos and other images are hung vertically, particularly if suspended the full length of the wall on a ribbon or hanging frame, they will make the room seem taller. When you hang images horizontally, the arrangement will tend to visually widen the wall. Too many images will make a room seem crowded. Balance and symmetry is always the rule.

Choice of housing for the wall display of collectibles is important, but it does not have to become complicated. For your collection of baskets, only a simple hanger need be attached to walls (or ceilings) to better display the collection. (A good use of space would be to store your yarn, seashell collection, or other objects in the baskets, provided the weight of these objects would not stress the wall or the basket.)

The idea is to be creative about your walls. They need not only support framed, printed images.

WORKING WALLS

Walls can work for you since they provide a great opportunity for lateral storage. Make the most of wall space by using shelving for storage, thus clearing up floor space. A narrow shelf at picture-rail height can be used to display decorative items. Bookshelves can be mounted to walls or fixed on casters so they may be moved away from the wall if need be. (Remember that books themselves make a strong decorative and emotional statement and you might want to consider concealed books if the idea of jumbles of volumes shakes you.)

Those with minimalist leanings may prefer to use wall space for additional closed cabinetry to hide electronics and other "essentials" of modern living.

Walls can dominate a room.

These questions will help you evaluate your existing wall situation, assess what you want, and what you need to change.

INTERIOR DESIGN: ELIZABETH READ WEBER, ASID, LLC

1. What is the basic condition of your walls? Are there cracks and rough places that need repairing before you apply decoration?

2. Which do you prefer—walls that are painted or walls that are papered? What are you living with now?

3. How do the walls contribute to the overall decorating scheme in the room? Are they the primary statement of style? Are they backdrops for your gallery of art?

4. If you change the walls in one room, what kind of effect will it have on adjoining rooms? Stand in one of the adjoining rooms and look through the doorway. How much of the walls can you see? Will your new idea clash with an existing palette?

5. Are there architectural elements or materials that you want to emphasize? Will painting or papering the walls around these elements hurt or help?

6. Do you have existing brick, metal, or stone walls that cannot be painted or papered?

7. Will simply changing the frames of the pictures or their organization on the walls give you a fresh, new look?

8. What existing color palette do you have to work from?

9. How much do you have budgeted for the changes in the walls?

10. Do you want to make the room appear larger? Will your color choice help you achieve that?

11. Will your wall decorating choice overpower your furniture? Is that intended?

12. Do you want to change all the walls or will changing one add the desired emphasis?

13. Have you considered papering the wall with a pattern or a texture? How will that change the room?

14. Consider the space. Will a screen or small wall help partition the room into more functional sections?

INTERIOR DESIGN: LILLIAN BOGOSSIAN AND VIVIAN WEIL, DECORATIVE INTERIORS; PHOTO: STEVE VIERRA

Section 2

FLOORS

Flooring in decorating is sometimes given limited attention, but today it is being given an expanded meaning—as a room's "fifth wall."

Not all the decoration for floors includes covering them. Many want to expose the floor is all its bare beauty.

THE GROUND RULE IN CHOOSING A FLOOR IS THAT IT be as good-looking as possible, because it will anchor your room and together hold its decorative scheme.

Flooring registers tactile sensations more than any other surface in the room because we step on it, so its importance to the look and feeling of your rooms should be considered.

Wood, along with stone, is the oldest building material for floors, and your home's floors are likely to be one or the other. Concrete flooring is used in some recently built homes and apartments, and many view covering it as the only option. However, when polished, it can be very modern and chic, and it can be "softened" to the feet with area rugs.

One important consideration when choosing flooring is to think of the relation of flooring in adjoining rooms. Make sure the transition in the types of flooring between rooms is not too jarring and that joins are neatly finished.

COLOR AND PATTERN ON FLOORS

When it comes to colors for floors many of us tend toward repeating color schemes we've seen under our feet outdoors. The area under our feet tends to feel comfortable in the green, brown, and black tones of the earth.

A desire for decorative flair may encourage you to think of using an unexpected color on your floors. But review the impact of color on space when selecting a floor coloring, because our perceptions of space are influenced by our perceptions of color. For example, oranges and reds on the floor tend to "shrink" a large room, while greens, blues and lilacs, which recede, will make a room appear "more spacious."

In applying color and patterns to the floor, conventional design strategy suggests that the scale of the patterns match those found elsewhere in the room. This is true whether the pattern has been painted onto the floor or is found in a carpeting or other types of floor coverings.

FLOOR MATERIALS THAT STAND UP

One of the most loved surfaces for homes, wood flooring today is more varied and versatile. Wood floors may be installed and cared for in most any room. But because wood shrinks and expands around moisture, it is not a good choice for bathrooms. For kitchens, wood stands up well when sealed against moisture. Both hardwoods and softwoods are used for flooring—with hardwoods being less likely to dent over time. Pine, oak, maple, and ash are the most common species used for flooring, although more exotic woods are available.

Existing wood floors in reasonable condition may be stripped and sanded—and bleached or stained for a stronger effect—before polishing.

If the floor is in a poor state, it can be painted or decorated and, in either case, be covered with a rug or two. Wood floors are durable and relatively easy to install and maintain.

Wood is available in strip, plank and parquet styles with strip being the more popular. Typically, it comes varying widths with tongue-and-groove pieces cut into random lengths. Parquet flooring, which forms repeating, mosaic patterns for a very formal lock, comes in pre-assembled tiles or interlocking pieces and can be laid according to manufacturers' directions.

Inlaid wood floors, like this one of walnut brittany designed by Suzan Santiago, add visual interest. Designs at our feet do not remain static. Geometric patterns at floor level will shift as the eye moves. PHOTO: KENTUCKY WOOD FLOORS

Waste not wood

When considering options for wood, you might consider recycled boards or boards reclaimed from old industrial or farm buildings.

Concrete is a basic building material for flooring that can, if left unadorned, appear sophisticated in some modern homes. A humble material, concrete has emerged as a simple, affordable flooring solution.

Essentially earth, concrete is a mixture of sand, water and cement powder. Concrete can and should be sealed and is resistant to stains and cracking. Polished, the surface may be left exposed for an elemental feeling. But because concrete forms a cold, heat-resistant floor, you may consider using it in rooms where a feeling of coziness is not a priority.

DECORATIVE COVERINGS FOR FLOORS

Paint, either solid or with special techniques such as stenciling or trompe l'oeil or other faux imagery, is a stylish option for floor decor.

Vinyl, sometimes maligned, has long been associated with practical flooring covering lacking in design punch. Today's offerings of color and design styles are wider, and the higher-priced vinyl flooring is low maintenance, non-allergenic, and durable under foot traffic.

Linoleum is not to be confused with vinyl. Linoleum is a sturdy floor covering made from a combination of natural raw materials including pine resins, linseed oil, wood flour, ground cork, and pigments pressed on a jute backing. It is static-free, relatively slip-free and sturdy for high-traffic areas.

Plastic laminates now used for floor covering act in much the same way as those for countertops. They are affordable, available in a wide range of colors, and easily maintained and installed. Laminates usually come packaged with in tongue-in-groove panels—the design varies with manufacturers. The joints should provide a tight, moisture-free seal for a floor covering that is suited for kitchens and baths. Wood and stone looks are available in laminates, as are matching borders.

Tiles on floors have a reputation for leaving the feet cold and the room feeling "hard." In some areas, baths and mudrooms, you might want a surface that is easily cleaned and relatively smooth to the surface. Rugs can be use to compensate when patches of "warmth" are required. Tiles can also be used in combination with other types of floor coverings.

Stone floors are durable and easily maintained. They can also be dramatic when used as the focal point of a room. Interior Design: Tomar Lampert Associates

Tiles can be made from fired clay or natural materials such as stone, slate and marble. Choose the colors of the tiled floor to blend or contrast with other colors in a room. All these elements in the tiles' appearance—material, finish, texture, color, shape, size, and pattern, must relate to the function and style of the room.

Natural fibers, such as sisal, coir, and seagrass, are among the least expensive floor coverings and provide a neutral, nubby base for most furniture styles. Remember that some straw and grass mats deteriorate if they are too dry so you may have to spritz with water occasionally.

Sisal is a strong, long-leaf fiber from the Mexican agave plant that has been elevated to designer status in the 1990s as the cravings for elements and materials that convey nature came into demand. As a result sisal can be can be more pricey than seagrass.

Of all the fibers, sisal is popular for its tailored texture that results from its being tightly woven (this can be scratchy to bare feet).

Sisal can be close-fitted like carpeting or made into loose laid mats or runners. Sisal is anti-static, hard wearing and relatively easy to keep clean. It comes latex or cotton-backed, in sun-bleached earth tones but can be expressively dyed colors.

Coir is a golden-brown fiber made from coconut palm. It is less expensive and less pliable than sisal but it is also stronger and will absorb really heavy wear.

Seagrass may include a variety of grasses that are usually woven into squares and sewn together.

Soft covering for floors

Carpeting, rugs, floorcloths, and other soft coverings for floors provide pleasant tactile as well as visual statements.

Carpeting can be like magic, adding instant, up-to-the-minute panache to a room. New color and texture underfoot can breathe new life into a space immediately and without effort.

Carpeting, like most decorative items, is subject to style and color trends. Carpeting that is "out of style" can quickly date a house. Remember the love-hate-love relationship we've had with shag carpeting?

But for its visual warmth and softness and ability to cushion our steps and help to eliminate unwanted sound, carpet retains a unique place in our hearts and homes.

Light-colored wood floors reflect light and provide a warm, lustrous backdrop for furniture. Interior Architecture: Olson Lewis & Dioli Architects; Photo: Eric Roth

Floor Accents

Sisal, raffia, and some coir matting may be given dash by attaching a border of fabric or by paint and stenciling.

If you'd like to cover a large area of a floor too big for a rug, you may simply reconsider the old notion of carpeting extending "wall to wall" and use special fasteners that would safely and discreetly secure the carpeting where you desire.

Carpeting is sold in three main varieties, though there are many weaving specialties and carpeting found in many regions around the world. Commercially, these three varieties include:

1) Cut pile, which has with yarn loops sheared at the top.

2) Loop pile, which leaves the yarn uncut and has a tight, compact weave.

3) Cut and loop, which combines both.

Nothing to sneeze at

Carpet fibers are usually made of nylon, polyester, polypropylene, or traditional wool or wool blends. Those concerned with allergies should be encouraged to investigate what kind of fibers are used in the carpeting. If carpeting is to be used in some intimate space, be wary of the toxic impact that artificial fibers can have. Natural wool may be the better choice.

Rugs and floorcloths, if they are bold in color, pattern, shape, or texture, can become the focal point of a room around which all the other decor revolves.

Contemporary artisans and craftspeople who have long employed ancient weaving techniques provide a wide variety of styles and options in rugs and floorcloths at retail that are truly works of art.

Rugs, which are really mini-carpets, offer the decorator a chance to introduce texture, color, and pattern in a more abbreviated fashion than would carpeting. Also, because some of the rugs of finer quality are made of linen or the softest wool, as are those in Persian and Turkish rugs, and thus are expensive, small versions make them affordable to more people.

Dhurries, rag rugs and kilims are also decorative coverings for floors that add texture and spirit without great expense.

Fancy (fantasy) flooring

Stone is among the many materials for creating something special underfoot. Stone floors can be costly, but they are an elegant and extremely long-lasting investment.

Granite and marble are popular choices for entryways, formal rooms, and at times, kitchen and dining areas—wherever a look of luxury is desired.

Quartz-based granite, which has a speckled appearance, is resistant to water, scratches and acids from citrus products such as oranges. Marble is more easily scratched. Both should be sealed and polished to maintain their luster. Low-gloss finishes will better hide dirt and footprints than will high gloss.

Stone and tiled floors provide a warm, sturdy feeling to this kitchen. Though costly to install, it is a good investments since a stone floor is durable and easily maintained. INTERIOR DESIGN: MEADOWBANK DESIGNS INC.

W ORKBOOK

FIGURE OUT
WHAT'S UNDERFOOT

Use these questions to help you think about important design decisions concerning your floors.

PHOTO COURTESY OF MILLING ROAD

1. What is the basic condition of your floors? Should you consider structural improvements before you consider decorative choices? What are these changes? New planks? A new floor poured to increase sound-proofing?

2. What do you expect from your floors? What type of wear and tear will be expected? What is the room's use and what type of floor covering will work best with that function? Is your floor going to see children and pets constantly? Will the room be entered only on special occasions?

3. How much money should you invest in flooring and floor coverings? Base your decision on price, wear and tear, upkeep and comfort (even to bare feet).

4. What type of material would you like underfoot? Materials such as stone, concrete and granite are durable, but what "feeling" would these materials introduce into a room. Would carpeting or some softer covering give your floors the "feeling" you want in this space?

5. After considering material, ask yourself about color and pattern? Do you want the floor to be the background of the decorative scheme or would you like for it to make the primary statement?

6. What is the relationship to this floor with the floors in the adjoining rooms? How could you make the floors seem to flow smoothly from room-to-room?

INTERIOR DESIGN: ELIZABETH READ WEBER, ASID, LLC

INTERIOR DESIGN: MANIJEH EMAY; PHOTO: STEVE VIERRA

Section 3

WINDOWS

Dressing a window or leaving it bare is not the only decorating decision you must make about windows.

Bare or there is a matter of personal choice but what the window wears will affect the mood of the room.

WINDOWS ARE OFTEN FIRST THING NOTED UPON ENTERING A ROOM —particularly if there aren't any. Designers and architects encourage generous use of windows for creating both warmth and an airy feeling of space and to allow in as much natural light as possible.

A window is our porthole onto the world, equal parts architecture and decoration. There are many considerations beyond "Do the windows open?"—an odd though familiar reality for urban apartment dwellers for whom windows aren't always an open-and-shut case.

Some windows should remain shuttered if the view is unsightly.

Windows let in light and air, shut out the cold and are a house's most distinctive exterior feature. When considering windows as part of your decor, think not only of decorating style but of the panes themselves.

If the windows gaze upon something outside that is particularly lovely, dressing would detract from this view.

If there are unique features about your windows themselves, you may not wish to cover them up. You may want to make those features a special thought in your decorating.

The windows in our homes are the ones we're stuck with unless you want to make capital improvements. But if you find that you're unhappy because your windows are too small or don't match, there are some visual tricks you may use to change what you don't like about your panes.

Windows that are small can be made to look bigger by painting the framework white.

Adding fabric dressings to tiny windows tends to visually shrink them further. But paneled shutters and louvered blinds seem to broaden the lines of narrow, smallish windows.

What a window sees and how we see it shapes our views of the window and its dressings in decor. Creative shape and placement of windows is sometimes the only decoration necessary. PHOTO: ROBERT PERRON

A Light Touch for Windows

For simple window treatments using
rods and rings, panels or lengths of soft
sheer fabric are ideal.

Sheers, which had been long out of
fashion, are enjoying a renaissance in
decorating. Sheers are often hung as
the lone dressing in windows of modern, minimalist interiors. Sheers of old
were stiff and made of synthetics but
many of today's sheers are translucent
and billowy and enhance light quality
through a window being made of natural fibers like cotton batiste, organdy, or
chiffon. When hung with extra fullness,
sheers may provide the same degree of
privacy as heavier fabrics without
reducing sunlight. Be generous in the
number of panels and the length of the
sheers, if used alone, so they may pud-
dle on the floor or be tied back, draped,
or looped. For an elegant look, drape
and loop white muslin over a plain
wooden rod and let it cascade down
both sides of the window to the floor.

If shutters and blinds are not options, perhaps some other decorative device
would work—stained panes, or using the window as a stage for displaying a collection of unusual objects—perhaps seashells or glass bottles. (Objects that
reflect light, when placed in window, add an interesting decorative sparkle to
those viewing them from both inside and outside of the house.)

Windows that are tall look good when dressed in just about everything. But
roman shades and blinds give them a lean, clean neatness.

Valances or a similar over-the-window treatment will bring the eye above the
window (giving the perception of even greater height to the overall room).

Floor-length draperies or fitted fabric screens can provide additional heat
insulation and can be pulled back when this is not required. Curtains of fine fabrics have ample space to hang and drape in tall windows.

Windows that are large or unusually shaped like "picture windows" seem to
defy most fabric dressings and look good outfitted in fitted blinds or shutters.
However, in some instances, lighter fabrics such as muslin and lace can be
draped over a picture window to allow light and the view.

Unusually shaped windows, such as Palladian windows, are difficult to dress
because of their shapes, and typically require custom-made curved draperies.
These special drapes should be hung high above the arch and allowed to cascade to the floor for the best look. For arched windows, and others, the
draperies or fabric panels may be suspended from the ceiling on a steel rod.

A bank or wall of windows should probably be treated as one window rather
than a series of related ones. (In making fabric choices for large windows,
remember that tiny prints tend to be lost in large spaces.)

Windows that don't match in size or function in a room present a special decorating challenge, but professionals discourage using more than one type of
dressing or window treatment in this case. The problems of asymmetry and proportion in rooms with windows differing in size and for rooms with windows and
large patio doors or French doors may be resolved with color or type of window
dressing. Working with fabric or other materials in the same color and texture
for all windows is one way of relating the windows to each other and the rest
of the room. For a simpler, cleaner looks, use blinds or shutters in all the same
color to unify the windows.

Window "furniture"

- Valances are window toppings that are soft, made completely from fabric. Valances draped over the curtains convey drama and opulence.
- Cornices are hard, shaped window toppings, usually made from wood or plastic and then covered with fabric to complement the curtains.
- Lambrequins are like cornices but also have arms that reach down either side of the window.

Adding windows? When adding windows or contemplating "picture windows," consider the rhythm of the interior space and the view from that window. Picture windows make a nicely framed view and provide a dramatic focal point, but they should be installed with discretion because they diminish privacy and are difficult to dress.

You will want to begin to furnish your windows with a mind towards the room's function and the amount of light received, giving a nod to the architecture of your home and the framework of the windows.

Window dressings can be a buffer and balance between the inside and outside, offering privacy and protection from weather. When properly placed, windows can unify or enhance the perception of a room. Dressing or not dressing the window is about framing the outside view as much as it is about coordinating the curtains with the rest of the room.

Help for blinds

For large windows where you want to use blinds, it looks better if you use several blinds or shades instead of one long one. This also gives you better light control in the room.

Dressings for windows

Windows should wear dressings that accentuate their best attributes, provide some warmth, and a degree of disguise. Wardrobes for windows should be stylish, flexible, and, where possible, easily cleaned.

In dressing a window, remember that less is usually better than more. Puffy, dramatic draperies can weigh down a design scheme and make you feel hemmed in. In thinking of dressings, choose either a minimal treatment or a formal treatment. Fabric and choices will add to your decor and visual impact to the room.

The quality and intensity of the light through the windows should be considered first in your thoughts about window dressings. Fabrics of varying weights can diffuse light, making the colors in sunlight lighter, richer and warmer than during evening light. This may affect your color choices. If the natural lighting through the window is low intensity, try some of the fabrics that have superior light-filtering qualities that enhance light.

Quality fabrics fall and drape with substance and softness. They may be substantial and crisp but never stiff. Never skimp on the fabric for windows because floor-length drapery benefits from a generous mass of fabric.

As you become more comfortable selecting window dressings, you may begin to experiment with fabric choices and styles. Assembling different colors, patterns and textures works well. Remember opposites attract: Brocade and muslin, velvet and sheers. But the fru-fru might not be for you. Choices in fabrics abound, as do other innovative ideas for dressing up a window.

Many stores' offerings of ready-made curtains are traditional heavy tapestry, damask, and brocade, though great amounts of them are needed and should be considered an investment. Most finely crafted fabrics do age well.

What style for your windows?

In choosing a style for your window dressings, its important to remember that the lines are important.

The window should influence your choice, and most professionals follow a simple rule: drapes should fall to the length of the floor or stop at the windowsill to avoid odd symmetry.

Roman shades and even the classic white roller shades provide another option for decorative detail in windows. In this sunfilled garden room inspired by British Indian style, shades also provide easier control over light. INTERIOR DESIGN: HORNE INTERNATIONAL DESIGN, INC.

Curtains that are richly tailored and deliberate with valances and palmets add distinctive, almost architectural details. The taller your ceiling the better for this type of treatment.

Curtain and drapery are essentially interchangeable terms, but technically, draperies are made of heavier fabric with greater tailoring, and curtains are fashioned to be easily opened and pushed aside.

A style of drapery is determined by its heading: that gathering at the top of the curtain. Headings are typically found in these styles:

- French or pinch pleats: have small clusters of three pleats groups at regular intervals
- Pencil pleats: are tighter than French and run continuously across the fabric (best on soft fabrics)
- Cartridge pleats: have formal, elaborate with stiff cuffs
- Smocked headings: look as if the gathers have been embroidered

For those interested in elaborate, formal window dressings there is also "furniture" for windows.

There are three different types of window "furniture" including valances, cornices and lambrequins. These are separate (wood or plastic) window coverings that are placed at the top of a window over the curtain hangings. All three are used to bring architectural distinction to room and provide a practical function of hiding hardware and attachments above the window.

LIGHT DRESSING FOR YOU?

One modern view in dressing windows is to forego fabric-laden designs in favor of those that provide decorative simplicity and ease of use and care.

Even if you prefer curtains, they can be simple. In keeping curtains simple, the decorative emphasis is placed on fixtures, such as interesting curtain rods or finials and tiebacks.

For a decorator's budget, this approach to windows provides considerable savings in rooms where formal draperies would be too expensive. What you save in fabric costs can be invested in another area.

If you decide to take the rod and finial route, then you may want to consider a simple fabric as well. In this case, fabric panels, sheers, and lace are preferred for their draping qualities.

Many retailers offer fabric panels that have rings or tabs at the heading and are opened and closed easily because they slide along a rod. This approach is unlike pinch pleat curtains, which require a traverse rod.

If you're starting out, don't rush to decide what your window wears. Buy the cheapest white paper roller blinds, which can be left as they are or painted, until you choose a more permanent design.

Blinds and shutters are among the more stylish means of dressing windows. Customized and available in all sorts of materials, blinds and shutters provide a neat, tailored look in this contemporary living room. INTERIOR DESIGN: KUCKLY ASSOCIATES, INC.

Curtain Inspirations

Using cafe clips and a little innovation, you can turn any bit of fabric into a curtain panel. Use the clips to snap around the fabric and slip the rod through the top. Anything from a piece or paper to last summer's beach sarong can become a window dressing.

WINDOW WRAPPERS

Some windows require more than a simple dressing, and the best options are fabric or paper screen coverings or shades.

Fabric screens customized to fit your windows can provide a measure of privacy but, depending on the fabric, you may sacrifice natural light or access.

Glass that has been sandblasted or etched, or treated with another decorative technique, may be your window choice. These may be installed as panes directly into the window, rested on the windowsill, or suspended from the ceiling to hang in proportion with the window.

Stained glass that is patterned presents its own focal statement in a room, so everything should probably respect that and try not to compete. Used in moderation, stained glass can add drama and mood contrast within your home. Stained glass is also quite heavy, so consider your window's framework before seeking installation. Also, when used directly as a window, some control over lighting and opening the window may be sacrificed.

JEWELRY FOR DRESSING WINDOWS

Rods and poles—of brass, wood, or steel—as well as finials provide a visual element and valuable function to hold fabric panels or paper attached to rings that slide along them.

Finials are the decorative tips that cap off the ends of each pole and are offered in decorating stores in many styles today from kitschy to sleek. They provide that extra sparkle, providing texture and detail that can make a room seem alive and pulled together.

Decorative tiebacks gracefully hold back the panels of your draperies. They also give you control over the amount of light you allow through the curtains.

Many are familiar with tiebacks that are hardware attached to the wall. Tiebacks—made of narrow bands of the matching panel or a contrasting fabric—can be used to tie the panel alone to create puffy, billowy looks. Where the tieback is placed can completely change the look of a window treatment, so try the tiebacks in several places before deciding or use differing placements as your mood changes.

Blinds, shutters and shades provide sleek looks, efficiency, privacy, and some noise control. The spare and lean looks are always practical and appropriate.

The tailored look of customized blinds and shutters always complements contemporary looks and modern architecture. Venetian blinds are recognized by their trademark two-inch cloth tapes and are still popular. Today's Venetian

INTERIOR DESIGN: MANIJEH EMAY; PHOTO: STEVE VIERRA

blinds are available in wood and painted aluminum as well the traditional cloth. Some blinds even come motorized and can be operated by remote control.

Technology has made it possible to customize blinds even for specialty windows including bay, picture, Palladian, and arched. Whether the blinds are vertical or horizontal is a matter of personal preference.

Among roller shades, white ones are, of course, classic, but many decorative and home centers have them in fabrics and decorative vinyl. Some are even available in gold mesh and taffeta.

Roman shades are graceful and operate on a simple cording system to draw up into a series of broad, flat folds. Unfolded, roman shades are somewhat boring, but become more interesting in this position when the roman shade's fabric is something softer, say organdy or silk.

Shutters inspire images of quaintness but wooden ones, when mounted to each side of the window frame (inside or outside), actually provide additional security and buffer unwanted, outside noises.

Typically made of hardwoods and often painted, shutters lend a strong decorative statement. If used on the exterior, consider their placement in context of the whole house's look. There are many styles of shutters, and the architecture of your home should dictate what style and color you choose. Most shutters are louvered to allow air and light control. If you want to try color, consider that the shutters could be the accent point, using a bolder hue than the body of house.

EXAMINE YOUR PANES, ROOM BY ROOM.

Windows are not easy to change in size or position, but there are lots of possibilities for fixing them up. Ask yourself these questions.

INTERIOR DESIGN: HORNE INTERNATIONAL DESIGN, INC.

1. How many windows are there? What type?

2. Is the glass clear, textured, colored, or stained?

3. What is the shape and style?

4. Are the windows shuttered? Should they be?

5. What is the quality of the light?

6. What are your needs for privacy and access to the window?

7. Is there something this window displays that you want to see? That you rather not see?

....

....

....

....

8. Record the dimensions for each window and note its position in the room.

....

....

....

....

9. Make choices, room-by-room on window dressings (or whether to leave them bare). Base these choices on privacy, need to access light and maintenance of the window treatments.

....

....

....

....

PHOTO: ERIC ROTH

Section 4

CEILINGS

YOUR PERSONAL PREFERENCES IN SPACE WILL DETERMINE WHETHER HIGH CEILINGS LEAVE YOU FEELING LOST OR FLYING FREE, or whether low ceilings feel cozy or claustrophobic. Generally, most people value a high ceiling in decorating, and ceilings rising higher than 10 feet are most desired and thought to make for a more gracious, serene space.

Still, ceilings, like floors, are often overlooked and under-explored for the decorative potential they hold. When you start to decorate a room, look up first to one of the room's largest uninterrupted surfaces.

Your decorating dilemma may be unhappiness with what's physically overhead. Are your ceilings too high or too low?

While there are some visual tricks professionals use to "raise" or "lower" a ceiling, if you desire dramatic physical changes, you may want to first determine whether structural changes can be made to the ceiling to achieve the look and feel that you desire.

For ceiling surfaces, the room's use and dimensions should be considered when planning the decorating scheme. In general, the higher the ceiling the more reason to give it some texture, depth and reflectiveness. Texture and pattern expand the horizons of walls and ceilings visually, creating a variety of moods and can provide an illusion of spaciousness.

LOOKING UP: WHAT DO YOU WANT TO SEE?

In choosing a decorative treatment for your ceiling, you will want to consider how much attention you want to attract away from the rest of the decor.

Painted ceilings can have surprising impact in a room. Even a coat of high-gloss paint will draw the eye upward in the room.

Applying color through paint, the decorator's indispensable tool, is the most versatile and inexpensive treatment for ceilings.

Colors for ceilings can follow the rules of the natural world outdoors. Most people are comfortable having a light value overhead and a dark value underfoot, and medium values around them.

A soaring ceiling can be a room's crowning jewel.

The real estate value can rise or fall on the height of "cathedral" ceilings or the detail of a ceiling's overhead beams or ornamental moldings.

Some people prefer to dwell in rooms that are open and airy with very high ceilings, while others prefer snug corners and rooms with a lower, ceiling.

A map of faux parchment was used for the ceiling of this library: the furniture, artwork, an antique Persian rug, and leather wall panels create a traditional, Old-World feeling of opulence. INTERIOR DESIGN: SUZANNE MCCALLEN/G.S.HINSEN COMPANYY

Ceilings too high, too low?

Designers use visual tricks when working in rooms with ceilings that are too low or too high.

- Vertical stripes on wallpaper or painted on walls help direct the gaze up and down, which seems to "raise" a low ceiling.

- Horizontal papers lead the eye around the room and makes the room appear smaller and brings the ceiling "down."

- A ceiling that is slightly darker than the walls makes the room appear to expand. (Extend the darker shade down the upper 12 to 18 inches (31 to 46 centimeters) of the wall and add molding to complete the effect.)

There are times when a white ceiling is preferred—white has aesthetic and light-enhancing benefits. White should be used when you'd like to focus all attention of a room's furnishings or some other part of the room's structure.

But don't resign yourself to basic shades because of fear or confusion. You may begin simply by reversing the color combination in a room. For example, if you have a room with yellow walls and a white ceiling, reverse the colors. An all-white interior, for example, can be exciting when topped by a boldly colored ceiling. The effect is a ceiling that is the lid on a wrapped box.

A fast-drying paint in a flat finish is the best choice for ceilings because glossy paint reveals the imperfections that inevitably show up as the surface settles over time.

If you are painting a whole room, you should begin with the ceiling, working away from the main source of natural light.

Painting your own sky on the ceiling of a room is one of the decorative motifs often interpreted by designers. Others paint stars or clouds to encourage visitors to gaze.

Decorative techniques for applying paint can be used on ceilings and as they are on walls and floors. Painting techniques such as trompe l'oeil and faux painting will draw attention. Be careful if it is not your desire to have the ceiling become the decor's focal point. As with all decorative elements, think about the ceiling in relation to all the room's other offerings.

Architectural details overhead may be highlighted by paint. Molding painted in a contrasting color is one way of adding interest at ceiling height, especially if the walls and ceiling are painted the same color.

Paper can be applied to ceilings as it is to walls and can be a creative visual effect. Commercial wallpaper or any paper-like material can work.

You will want to choose a pattern or color that differs from the wall's (if you're papering them as well) to avoid a "boxed in" feeling that will be created by being surrounded by a repeating pattern on all sides.

Ornamented ceilings such as old-fashioned pressed tin or ornamental plastering are uplifting and convey history and tradition. Most ornamental ceiling choices are rough-hewn wood, plaster moldings, thin beading and silver and aluminum leaf. Adventurous decorators will experiment with all types of ornamentation that could possibly work on ceilings. A lattice-work trellis cut to fit the ceiling overhead can add a wistful touch to a garden or sun room. You might even like to hang a flower or two or lace a ribbon through it.

A sun porch/informal dining space was treated to a top of trellis-inspired woodwork. Garden trellises can become a creative decorator's materials for all surfaces including a ceiling. Pay attention to weight of material and how much visual attention you want to create above. INTERIOR DESIGN: KLINGMAN'S OF GRAND RAPIDS.

Noise Control

For noise control and other visual sleeping aids, designers suggest looking heavenward. Does your ceiling provide opportunity to buffer sound if you applied acoustical tiles? Will you child fall asleep by counting the sheep painted overhead? Or will she feel safer if Barney is papered overhead?

Fabrics and natural fibers of the same type as used on walls can add interesting texture and visual drama to ceilings. In a monochromatic room, a billowy, romantic ceiling may be created by stapling "clouds" made from puffy gatherings of soft fabrics such a voile or organdy, repeating this effect until the entire ceiling is a billowy topping on a space. The fabric must be light and pliable for the desired effect.

Natural fibers such as seagrasses and woven raffia may also be used effectively overhead to create texture and provide a neutral background for a lighting fixture or some other decorative element.

Ceiling as storage space may have some positive decorative elements. Ceiling space for storage may appeal to you if have collectibles or objects that you would not mind have hanging overhead. Of course, be aware of the weight of the object and the amount your ceiling may safely support.

SPEND SOME TIME LOOKING AT YOUR CEILING.

Use these questions to discover your preferences.

INTERIOR DESIGN: DIAMOND BARATTA DESIGN, INC.

1. What shape is the ceiling?

2. Enter the room looking straight ahead. How much of the ceiling can you see?

3. What kinds of activities are performed in the room? Would a dark or light ceiling be most advantageous?

4. Consider the size of the room. A bright ceiling will keep a room large, a dark ceiling will make the room feel smaller and cozier. Which do you desire?

5. A high ceiling will benefit from some texture. Is your ceiling over twelve feet up?

6. Are their architectural details on your ceiling that could be emphasized?

7. Consider how much attention you want to attract away from the rest of the decor. What is the current focal point of the room?

INTERIOR DESIGN: SUZANNE MCCALLEN/
G.S. HINSEN COMPANY

INTERIOR DESIGN: LISE DAVIS DESIGN AT JAMES BILLING ANTIQUES AND
INTERIORS; PHOTO: PETER JAQUITH

Section 5

PASSAGES

The foyer or entry
hallway is the first
impression that a
visitor gets of the
house and is probably
the most lasting.

Entryways and
receiving halls serve
a fundamental role
to all who enter: they
are places to pause in,
before moving on to the
rich interior life of the
rest of the house.

FIRST IMPRESSIONS OF A HOME ARE MADE UPON ENTER-ING. A dim and dingy entryway, no matter how sparkly the rest of the house, creates a depressing atmosphere.

In general, to experience a clear difference from the outside to the inside, one must feel immediately cushioned upon entering.

Even those in a small living space should resist the temptation to enlarge the room by getting rid of the entry hall. It seems like a good idea but in the psychological sense it is very disconcerting to step directly from the street into the living room. Aside from reducing privacy and sacrificing the ceremony of entry, everyone who enters your home loses that brief opportunity to mentally adjust to entering a new space.

The entry must function efficiently for you and your visitors as a place to pause, put down packages, keys, and coats and check the mirror.

If you want to have an "inviting" home, then a cozy entryway is in necessary. If you prefer to "distance" guests, a more formal treatment of the entrance hall may be required.

But often entryways and hallways are the most difficult parts of the house to decorate. Lack of light and high traffic are among the larger decorating issues. You need to find decorating schemes that will improve the feeling of light and space.

Doors should always be appropriate in size and spirit to the surrounding architecture. The way a door looks hints at what may lie beyond. Doors introduce and, sometimes, invite us into rooms. Large doors seem to suggest spirited interaction, while smaller doors hint at quiet intimacy.

The front door sets the spirit of your home. The grander the home, traditionally, the more elaborate the entryway.

Primary entrances (with or without a porch) should be well lighted for safety and for helping create a feeling of expectation and welcome.

The front door and all exterior doors are required to meet federal standards for safety and access. Shop carefully when replacing exterior and interior doors, making yourself aware of the best features.

Nestled above a doorway, a generously oversized contemporary transom with a pane of etched glass filters light into a stairwell. Patterned after a chambered nautilus, this shell is clear plate glass with etched details and background.

Photo: Robert Perron

Which colors say welcome?

The best color for a foyer is a light or bright one. Avoid dark colors unless the foyer is very large. Good creative lighting can enhance a dark entryway. Architects also suggest low ceilings in the entrance/foyer to maximize the perspective of the space that stretches beyond. Again, the foyer should be well-lit to seem inviting and "safe."

Details for doors

To ornament your front door, consider all the varieties of decorative hardware available. Handles and hinges could add a dazzle to a drab door. Choose a new outer doorknob and outside accessories.

In terms of styling, always consider the age and style of your home. Unless you have a home style that would support them, avoid glass and heavy metal doors. If your house is simple, the front door should be, too. Always consider the weight and the door handles, as well as the door knocker or whatever door-answering system you choose.

A front doors may be distinguished by paint or its natural materials. Front doors are usually painted in a color contrasting with the color of the body of the house. Which color you choose should be personal favorite. If you like fuschia, why not try it on the front door?

Legendary decorator Elsie de Wolfe, a pioneer during the start of the design profession, scandalized Manhattan society in the 1900s by painting a front door firehouse-red enamel. Bold color for front doors can be used as dramatically today but likely without such alarm.

Front doors can become display space for arts and crafts or greenery. (Exterior decor should be considered as you would interior looks. Flags, wind chimes and baskets should of the same quality and design spirit as the rest of your home; sometimes "cute" looks cutesy.)

Interior doors sometimes interrupt the flow of rooms, but to control traffic and protect privacy, doors are often necessary.

Doors and frames needs not suffer decorative boredom, but their design purpose is primarily one of function. Painting the door and the frame different colors sets them apart and provides subtle decorative detail (it the colors are harmonious).

Painting a door dark in a room of light palettes defines it architecturally and can provide surface for decorative paint treatments.

Door makers also sell a range of trims and decorative options to accompany their door styles. You might also try hanging swags of fresh or dried florals and greens over your doors to add seasonal flavor.

If your home has long vistas, use them to advantage: You may elect to keep palettes and materials light and use the walls to display framed images or special furnishings. PHOTO: JOHN M. HALL

Storage space

Your doors can become additional storage space for you. For behind-the-door storage, a shoe bag or one fashioned from vintage fabric becomes a charming catch-all for letters, pencils, photos, and others odds and ends.

Architecturally, hallways serve as breathing spaces between rooms. As such, this hall space should be kept relatively free of clutter.

If your hallway is wide enough for furniture but is unlikely to be used as a sitting area, it is perhaps best to display furniture that is purely decorative.

Or consider using the hall's wall as a gallery for display of collectibles or favored framed images.

Ideally, since so many other rooms open off hallways you'll need to find some way of linking the design to those other rooms, perhaps by repeating either color, schemes or repeating the floor covering throughout the space. If your home has long interior vistas, plan the progression of color from room to room so that the whole house appears to work together.

Use the same sorts of colors and textures in connecting such areas such as hallways and stairs, using the same family of basic materials for surfaces and finishes and avoiding abrupt aesthetic leaps from style to style. This will bring a sense of coherence to a sequence of rooms and help to define the essence of a home.

Most hallways have a large number of doors opening off them. One solution is to finds ways of making an interesting feature of them. Perhaps you could stencil borders around the architrave (top) or by giving the doors attractive paint finishes.

Neutral or light colors work best in hallways because they make the best use of limited lighting available in these areas. Try to avoid heavily patterned or dark wallpapers or paint treatments in hallways because they will shrink the space and might present a gloomy, overbearing impression.

Plan your hallway lighting according to use and the mood you'd like to create. For example, if you want to display artwork, spot or track lighting might work best and provide high-quality light. In hallways between bedrooms, a softer, muted lighting could be used to maintain the atmosphere of relaxation.

Stairways can become major design features, something akin to sculpture, in modern, architecturally driven homes.

Places of transition in your homes, such as the ends of hallways, the space above the landing, are useful for the display of special objects. Space where you only spend seconds should be exciting to pass through, consider placing favorite collections there. INTERIOR DESIGN: SISTINE INTERIORS

Decorated doors

If you are interested in paper crafts, consider using decoupage for interior door decoration.

But for most of us, stairways are purely functional part of our standard home design—a means from getting from one floor to another.

The average stairway is usually dowdy if not downright ugly. At best, a coat of paint is the most decorative treatment given stairways. So beyond replacing a banister, it is probably a matter of deciding whether to strip, paint or polish the wood of the existing staircase.

Stairways, like floors, need to be durable and washable. You should consider the period and character of your home before deciding on the material for stairs.

As for stair treads, if they are in good condition and are of elegant proportion, it is a loss to hide them under carpeting. Bare trends, nonetheless, are noisy, so a good compromise is a runner. If you desire to cover each of the stair treads, one clever decorating trick is to alternate the color and/or patterns of carpeting on each of the steps.

Throughways and tiny odd spaces, those nooks and passageways throughout your house where you spend only seconds at a time, are tiny treasures.

At entrances, on stairs, and along hallways are spaces that have special impact and when decorated to please all the senses, throughways may provide pockets of good feelings throughout your home.

In the language of Zen Buddhism, if there are windows, these "places of transition" in our living space may offer us glimpses at the outside. If the spaces are contained, they could become the place for objects of our desire.

Some passageways may be large to become really functional space for solitary activities. For example, a window seat could be installed at the end of a hallway that receives early morning light. The landing at the top of the stairs, if there is enough space for a comfortable chair and table, can become a nice quiet place for some reading.

This stairway, in all its bare beauty, became the the center of attention in an old farmhouse remodeled by Tommy Simpson. If the wood of your stairs is special perhaps you should let its interior beauty shine.

PHOTO: ROBERT PERRON

Narrow halls

Installing a picture rail or molding about 3/4 up the length of the walls will help to "reduce" the height of a particularly high-ceilinged hall and will also help it to appear wider.

WORKBOOK

PRETEND THAT YOU are a first-time visitor. The entryway will set the tone for your own home. These questions will allow you to take a fresh look at your entryway.

1. Walk into your entry hallway from the outside. What kind of feeling do you get? Do you seem to have enough light? Does the entry seem crowded? Dark? Dank?

2. Is it welcoming? Does it look lived in or very formal? Is there any "breathing space" between entering your home and stepping into the first major room? Entryways work best when they seem a separate "weigh station" before passing into the rest of the home? How can you create this effect if you have no foyer? Could you use a screen or room divider to create a separation from the street to the first room?

3. Does the style and furnishings in the entryway reflect what can be found in the rest of the house or is it jarringly different? Why is that?

4. Is it well lit? What areas could be better lit?

INTERIOR DESIGN: CANN & COMPANY; PHOTO: ERIC ROTH

PHOTO: TIM STREET-PORTER

5. Is there a lot of clutter? Are their deadspaces that you could turn into easy storage areas?

6. Is the entryway functioning properly? Is it immediately evident where guest and residents can put their coats and belongings? Is the coat rack inhibiting movement? Is there a better place to put it?

7. Mirrors help enlarge a space, and are convenient for a last minute check before you leave. Is there a place for a mirror near your door?

251

Chapter 4

ALL
Together

DECORATING A ROOM, or an entire home, is a personal expression of who you are. Magazines and experts suggest we adapt and re-create trappings of "lifestyle" concepts that may not make you feel at home. What we can learn from others is how they put together the elements to serve their needs and satisfy their decorating style.

Mastering the art of shaping a home around our individual and family styles instead of following fashion can lead to domestic well-being. Take a look at how some great rooms work and come together.

The cool, modern architecture in this dramatic space provides a great space for a spiraling stairwell. Stairwells work best when allowed room to express their design integrity. INTERIOR DESIGN: OLSON LEWIS & DIOLI ARCHITECTS; PHOTO: ERIC ROTH

Section 1

BEDROOMS

SINCE WE TRY TO CRAM FAR TOO MANY FUNCTIONS INTO THEM—dressing and toiletry and general storage and work space—bedrooms fulfill none of them particularly well. We've come to demand so much more from our bedrooms as entertainment and centers of computers and business.

Where possible, shift the emphasis of some of these functions to other rooms. If space is a premium, perhaps combining beds and business is efficient, but to enhance relaxation and a peaceful aura, bedrooms should be retained for relaxing and sleeping.

Before you starting decorating your bedroom, ask yourself questions regarding your space and function needs. What do you use this room for? The purpose may seem obvious, but be realistic about which activities you'd really like to keep in the bedroom and which would serve you better elsewhere. If you're going to combine many activities in your bedroom, you will need to keep the furnishings streamlined and minimal to avoid a cluttered look.

Other questions might include: Do you really need the largest room? Would the children be better served by greater space offered by the "master" bedroom? Where should bedrooms be located? Many people feel uncomfortable with bedrooms on the ground level of a dwelling, but this may be practical for ease of movement for older inhabitants.

What storage needs do you have for the bedroom? Objects have visual energy in the room, so try to limit the number of items you choose to store or display in bedroom. Beds, are, of course, the largest furniture feature in a bedroom.

One solution, if you want a bedroom of dual function, is to think of buying a bed on casters that can be moved during the day to create needed space.

The bed, inevitably, is the visual focus of the bedroom, but comfort is what makes it inviting. Invest in a good mattress. Get a bed large enough to accommodate the sleeper(s).

Because the bed makes the largest single statement, you may not want one that is characterless. Bedframes of differing styles can conjure different emotions. A four-poster bed is associated with romance. If a canopy is added, mood shifts to one of tradition with imagery of historical significance. Wood, iron, and steel are the primary material sources for bedframes.

Bedrooms should be relaxing.

This should not be considered an impossible dream.

Bedrooms present a special design and space challenge.

254

This bedroom is designed for the basic activity of sleeping but many other activities are done in modern bedrooms—dressing, entertaining and yes, even business. Is your bedroom designed for soundest sleeping? INTERIOR DESIGN: VICENTE WOLF ASSOCIATES

Making space to sleep

Split a large living room into a sitting and sleeping area with screens, freeing a small bedroom for other purposes. In Japan, it is the norm to have a movable bed —a futon, usually—that can be rolled up in the morning and put out of sight. Hammocks can be used in the same efficient fashion.

Decorator headboards

Reconsider conventional headboards: Scavenging through flea markets or architectural salvage depots and auctions may yield great items with decorative possibilities. The bed is actually a frame that holds the mattress. Reclaiming a headboard can be fun and inexpensive. An old mantelpiece can be transformed into a headboard simply by filling in the opening with upholstery or a wallpaper screen.

Headboards, which are separate from the bed's frame, are wonderful decorative opportunities. Headboards work best when place against the wall rather than allowed to float in space.

The position of the bed is usually determined by the room's longest uninterrupted wall space. Psychologically, many people have been said to prefer a bed catercorner to the door. This positioning is emphasized also by practitioners of feng shui, the Chinese art of placement. This position—half concealed behind the door—is best for beds because the sleeper can see anyone who enters the room before being seen.

A bed requires little other furniture, but the decorative necessities are a headboard tall enough for reading and a bedframe that has no sharp edges to snag legs or linens.

Chests of drawers and sidetables are also often used for storage and convenient access to tabletop lighting and personal items. Beds and chests of drawers are the largest items in the house and they're usually crammed into one of the smallest rooms, so when adding furniture other than a bed, beware. Less is usually more relaxing.

By simply dressing the bed you will begin to give the room its decorative flavor. Once you've chosen a bed or frame you can "dress it up" with a canopy or by draping hangings from the ceiling or leave it undressed, wearing on its basic bedclothes—sheets, pillowcases, and blanket or comforter.

Bedrooms have historically tended to be colored yellow or white, for the light enhancing qualities of those hues. Approach your colors in the bedrooms as you do in the rest of the house—as a personal choice. Some prefer the soothing palettes of pastels and neutrals, while others find that a splash of bold color is a treat to wake up to.

Much is demanded of a bedroom's "eyes." The windows and their dressings must serve many roles. At night, they should add to the atmosphere of comfort and privacy, but by day they should allow morning's bright light.

Ideally, your curtains or shades should echo some part of the other soft furnishings. You want to avoid really heavy fabrics because they carry much visual "weight" and may tend to make a bedroom feel claustrophobic.

ARE TELEVISIONS BAD DECORATION?

Designers and home decorators fret when it comes to the trappings of our technology-driven world. But where do they make the most attractive use?

Most homes have personal electronics in all rooms. Decorative considerations regarding electronics have to be made depending on the function of the space. In the "living room" or the "den" or "family room," there is not much need to disguise the presence of televisions or recreation equipment.

In other rooms, bedrooms, for example, you may not want view the electronic device when it is not in use. Many cabinets and bookcases are available that provide a cover or door for camouflage.

Music systems, fortunately, have become more streamlined and have been designed to be less obtrusive in a room's decor. State-of-the-art systems come with speakers that are neat, compact and provide little visual disturbance.

Office equipment is very obvious, and it's difficult to hide its function or its wiring. Finding the best desk or housing for the monitor and its parts is wise. For decoration? Simply covering the machine with fabric or plastic coverings is about as good as they're going to look.

As the largest piece in the room, the bed defines the decorative spirit. This contemporary four-poster bed with a graceful canopy may inspire in you sweeter sleep.
PHOTO: ROBERT PERRON

Good sleep

We sleep more soundly and deeply when all the senses are soothed, with fresh air and cool breezes that calm us at night and natural light that wakes us gently in the morning. Although many have grown fond of air-conditioning, ceiling fans provide air movement and a pleasant sound.

ROOM FOR YOUR BED

There are many things to consider when decorating a bedroom. Use these questions to guide you.

1. What furniture do you have in the bedroom? Is it cluttered? Would it help to move these pieces out of the room?

2. Consider the activities you mostly do in your bedroom. Does the furniture in the room reflect these activities or is there excess? Which parts of the room are you satisfied with? Which are you dissatisfied with? Why are you dissatisfied with these areas?

3. What organization of personal possessions would make the room seem less cluttered?

4. What is the quality of lighting in your bedroom? Is it conducive for both relaxing and working? How can you change or add simple things like reading lamps that ensure adequate lighting for all tasks?

5. Is your choice of decoration "healthy" for the bedroom? You want to consider how the draperies, floor coverings and bed linens might hold dust and dirt and might be affecting the quality of air and light in the place where you relax.

6. Does the color of your bedroom jar or calm you? What type of wallcovering makes you feel most cozy?

7. What color might make the space seem more sensual? Which bed coverings would make you want to climb under them? Would no coverings at all suit you better? No bed at all, perhaps only a day bed?

INTERIOR DESIGN; SEARL DESIGN; PHOTO: PETER PAIGE

PHOTO COURTESY OF BRUNSCHWIG & FILS

Section 2

KITCHENS

Kitchen decor can
signal our attitude
about food preparation
or eating styles.

THE KITCHEN IS THE HEART OF MANY A WARM, INVITING
HOME. Long considered unsuitable for lingering, kitchens have evolved in architectural use from the purely functional "bowels" of a house into the spaces for
the most intimate of family gatherings.

In many modern homes concerned with efficient space use, the kitchen and
dining room have merged. This has created endless opportunities for decorating
that are not limited to the kitchen's primary culinary functions.

As domestic duties of cooking and cleaning become less associated with gen-
der, the lessening of negative cultural associations with the kitchen as being "a
woman's place" have liberated our considerations of the space.

Some people, for example, may prefer the look and feel of kitchen of stainless steel, high-quality appliances equipped with professional cooking tools that
would enhance the major function of the kitchen: cooking.

Others who might not be so interested in cooking might prefer simpler appliances, ranges with limited number of burners, electing to use the remaining
kitchen space to decorate, in, say, a farmhouse style, filling the room with cozy-
looking furniture and fixings.

Even you prefer a mix of both—state-of-the-art appliances and homey, "lived-
in" decorative looks—your choices are unlimited. (Except by budget, of course.)

If you have space, the best kitchens tend to follow what the French call "le
living." This is an open plan that suggests a layout for kitchens: Cooking appliances at one end with a chair or sofa in the middle and on the other end of the
kitchen's space is for storage and temporary storage of things for children and
pets who are visiting the room.

In this modern view of kitchens as social centers, the more lived in and loved
a kitchen appears, the less its primary function appears. Decorative objects that
have little to do with things culinary as well as comfortable, pretty furniture
could be added to the kitchen's decor for a more charming room.

**In a remodeled Victorian house, artisan Sandy Moore
replaced ordinary kitchen cabinet doors with the subtle
beauty of etched glass held in place by decorative wood
molding. Only the onion motif is left clear and the background etched, blocking the view of the cabinet's contents.
The process could be reversed to display the contents by
leaving more clear glass.** PHOTO: ROBERT PERRON

What shape is your kitchen?

- "Le living" or single line kitchens work best if you have more than 10 feet of running space. They should be planned carefully.

- L-shaped kitchens allow space for in-kitchen eating furnishing that do not interfere with the cooking, which should be planned for the opposite end of the room.

- U-shaped kitchens, which tend to be small, sometimes don't allow for in-kitchen eating. Consider flexible countertops (the kind that fold away when not in use) to give yourself extra space. Also, placing the refrigerator at the end of the longest running wall allows for easier access.

Think triangles

Professional designers of kitchens sometimes employ what is called a "work triangle," in planning where to place the major appliances. Ideally, an imaginary "triangle" can be drawn between the sink, range and refrigerator. For efficiency, two centers of work should be no more than two arm lengths apart. Nor should the members of this working triad be too close together as to cramp your movement.

In planning the space in your kitchen, the three fundamentals that you must consider are the positions of the cooking facilities, the sink, and the refrigerator. Once you've established this, the placement of other elements will be fairly easy.

Storage for your kitchen is the other component of space planning. You'll always need double what you think you will. Plan storage for the future gatherings, not simply what you must house now. Cabinetry and all sorts of organization systems are available for kitchens.

Group similar items—all pots, for example—in one place and organize them according to when they'll likely be used. If you only use the fondue cooker once a year, perhaps it could be stored elsewhere in the house rather than taking up valuable cabinet space. (Remember to continually edit and purge from your holdings to make sure you're housing only items that you'll really need or want in the kitchen.)

Custom-made kitchens may be very sophisticated, and sometimes costly, executed with professional assistance. If you are on a limited budget, you may want to think of more creative, decorative approaches.

Cabinetry is often the biggest design statement and largest investment in kitchen remodeling. Cabinets come in the following categories:

Stock cabinets can be purchased off-the-shelf in home centers.

Semi-custom cabinets refers to factory made cabinets that are custom ordered from a given number of door styles, finishes and sizes.

Custom cabinets are made by suppliers or at local shops to home owners specifications. Door styles usually influence the look, underscored by material and finish.

Storage and space-planning were key considerations in this "live-in" kitchen in an 1890s oceanfront cottage that was stripped to its studs and remodeled as a state-of-the art kitchen for a chef but remained true to the design period of the house. INTERIOR DESIGN: STEDILA DESIGN INC.

Raising the roof

Ceilings of different heights in the kitchen will seem to break up the space visually and create areas with a defined sense of their own while contributing to the whole space.

Sink placement

For decorative and emotional impact, it makes the best sense to position the sink underneath a window if there is one available. This is purely for emotional consideration of the dishwasher who would likely feel less "hemmed" in facing a window than facing a wall. Another favored position for sinks is facing outward into the room, located in an island or free-standing. For practical purposes, automatic dishwashers should also be placed near the sink.

White-washed?

Traditionally, white is considered the best color for kitchen because of its light enhancing qualities and its emotional associations with cleanliness. Also the neutral shade provides no competition with the natural coloring of foods.

The materials used for kitchen countertops and other work surfaces will add to the efficiency of the kitchen.

The many options for countertops and backsplashes include:

Laminates, popular countertop surfaces, are thin sheets of polymers usually installed over plywood underlay. Laminates are inexpensive, durable, easily maintained and provide an array of color choices.

Solid surfacing, such as acrylic and polyurethane-acrylic materials, mimic the look of expensive stone like marble and granite. Cheaper than using the actual stone or marble, these will not stain easily but can become scratched and burned by hot pots.

Stone, such as granite and marble, are popular choices for countertops, because they provide a solid, luxurious look. Granite is resistant to water, scratches and acids from citrus products such as oranges. Marble is more easily scratched. Both should be sealed and polished to maintain their luster. Low-gloss finishes will better hide dirt and fingerprints than high gloss.

Butcher block is made of oak or maple pieces glued together under pressure. Handsome and practical if you do a lot of chopping, but butcher block should never be installed near a sink because it will absorb water.

Unsealed butcher block must be seasoned with mineral oil before use and thereafter to prevent stains and prevent food particles and bacteria from becoming absorbed. Finishes are not recommended because they can chip.

Kitchens are being designed to combine multiple functions: cooking, eating, and socializing. INTERIOR DESIGN: NANCY MULLAN, ASID, CKD; PHOTO; RICHARD FELBER

Cabinet decoration

Cabinets may be covered with non-traditional materials. For example, a nice decorative touch could be to replace existing cabinetry with glass panes to add sparkle to a kitchen space.

EXPLORE THE MANY FACETS OF THE KITCHEN

Use these questions as a guide.

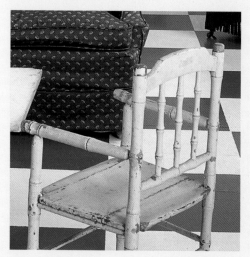

PHOTO: ERIC ROTH

1. What activites are performed in your kitchen? Cooking? Eating? Greeting guests? Family gatherings? Does your kitchen comfortably support all these activities? Can it support cooking and socializing at the same time? If not, are there space expansions that could be made?

---

2. How much value to you place on the appliances? Is a professional kitchen what you really need to satisfy your flair for gourmet cooking? Or can you get by with a two-burner range with no place for baking? What type of appliances do you have now? What don't you need? Never plug in the dishwasher? Perhaps you could consider using that space in another way.

---

3. Try to identify the working triangle in your kitchen. Are appliances and furnishings in the most ideal locations to make cooking and cleaning efficient?

---

4. In the decorative sense, does you kitchen make you happy? Are you bored with the cabinetry? What style of cabinetry would make you most happy? Would you rather have glass doors insteads of doors that hide shelf contents?

---

5. What type of furniture and entertainment items do you have? Do they suit all the activities that take place? What is needed to make this a real live-in, eat-in space or a stream-lined cooking operation, if that's what you'd prefer?

6. How can you change the floorcoverings, window dressings and wall decorations to make cleaning your kitchen less labor-instensive? A new flooring of scuff-proof laminate might work better than having to hand polish a hardwood floor? What's best and least cumbersome to maintain?

7. How could you better organize items in your closets and other areas for better storage? Have you allowed for future accumulation of items and utensils? Have you considered the walls and the space overhead for help in possible storage solutions?

Section 3

BATHROOMS

Bathrooms have changed from being purely utilitarian. After kitchens, they are the hardest rooms in the house to plan.

In planning a bathroom, space is your primary consideration. A bathroom needs to be at least as long as it is wide in order for comfortable use.

THE BATHROOM HAS BECOME ONE OF THE FAVORED ROOMS IN THE HOME. This attitude is not necessarily associated with a concern with cleanliness. Bathrooms represent private, introspective space as well as a place for hygiene in our increasingly crowded homes. For those also interested in decoration, this has opened up the bath to the same design considerations as other rooms.

Guest bathrooms, like living rooms, sometimes take a more ornate treatment, conveying greater style and status than your more functional bathing spaces. But how you decorate your bath is really among the most private matters.

There are three items that you must site—the bathtub/shower, toilet, and sink. There is likely more than one position, so plot on your floor plan all the possibilities. The position of your drainage and plumbing may suggest the placement of these features.

The longest wall makes the best placement for bathtubs, unless the room is long. In this case, the far end of the bath may be the best spot for the tub. In tiny baths, you may forego the tub in favor of a shower stall.

In a larger space, the bathtub may be placed in the center or in some other position that creates visual interest and helps you to "zone" the rest of the room with other furnishings that would provide for other uses.

The toilet should not be the first thing you see when you enter a bathroom. This requires forethought. Make sure there is enough room (at least 24 inches) between the rim of the seat and the wall in front so that your knees are not cramped when sitting.

The sink or wash basin should be placed with enough space in front of you so that you can comfortably bend over it. Ideally, you will have counter space for storage and holding toiletries.

Neutral colors provide a relaxing palette for this small but efficient bathing space. The dual sink basin and large mirrors make the bathing space able to accommodate more bathers at a time. Keeping with the spare decor, only decorative sconces and simple counter accessories introduce a "style" the bathroom. INTERIOR DESIGN: LESLIE JONES INC.

Sofas with your soap?

If you have the luxury of a large bath-room, or are remodeling to make larger bath, think of furnishing it as you would other rooms. Large bathrooms some-times leave "empty" space in the mid-dle after the plumbing needs have been taken care of. The answer may lie in adding furnishings such as comfortable, seating in water-resistant fabrics or by adding a dressing table or a small source of entertainment — books, music, or candles for meditation.

Covered storage for these toiletries should also be considered. Your sink could be set into a countertop surface with cabinets underneath for linens and so on.

Decorative details in the bathroom are sometimes defined by its fittings or fixtures. Basins and bathtubs are available in many styles and the fixtures should help convey their design spirit.

Because of their fairly restricted size, bathrooms can be satisfying to deco-rate. White and blue tiles are not your only options for wall and floor treatments, but tile and other materials such as stone and plastic laminates do provide durable surfaces that resist water and mildew.

Wall treatments should be simple and practical, with consideration given to how easily they can be cleaned and maintained. But there are many possibilities with coated wallpaper, stone, and paint to add visual interest.

Window-dressing in the bathroom may seem "overdone" and may, in some cases, not be hygienic. Fabric curtains absorb moisture. You may decide to do without curtains and instead use plain blinds or shutters to retain privacy. Shades allow great control over light and privacy in the bath without worry about effects of water on curtains. A shower curtain could be adapted for windows as well.

Good lighting, as close to natural as possible, is essential in bathrooms because of the importance of the grooming tasks performed there.

Accessories such as mirrors, artwork, and even linens, will help you complete your decorating plan or theme. Even soap dishes come in a variety of contem-porary designs.

Eliminate the need for bulky window treatments by incorporated safety glass or even trying obscure types of. Research options at your local glass shop.

PHOTOGRAPHY: ED GOHLICH

DESIGN: MARYCLARE BRANDT, ASID

(Above) With one-color tile, basics like sinks, shelving, and faucets become important visuals, and their unique shapes, colors, and textures are emphasized.

DESIGN: ARTHUR DE MATTOS CASAS

GETTING INTO THE BATH

Ask yourself these important questions about design and function in your bathroom.

INTERIOR DESIGN: AUSTIN PATTERSON DISSTON; PHOTO: ROBERT BENSON

1. Do you think of the bathroom as a place simply for hygiene or for solitary (or group) pampering and relaxing? Does your bathroom today meet that ideal?

2. Are there captial improvements that might make the bathroom among your favorite dwelling spaces? Would a shower or a hot tub make the space more to your liking? Consider the costs of such improvements, recognizing that this type of home improvement adds to the value of your home both monetarily and in real use.

3. How much space do you have in the bathroom? How much more would you like? Is it possible to remove the bathtub and replace with shower-only to create this new space?

4. What are you storage needs for the bathroom? Is this also your dressing room as well? Your family's? Devise a solution for storing items most needed during these grooming rituals. Perhaps a closet now holding cleaning supplies could be used as an area for access to vanity items.

INTERIOR DESIGN: LESLIE JONES. INC.

INTERIOR DESIGN: LESLIE JONES. INC.

5. How would simply changing the plumbing hardware or cabinetry give your bathroom a face-lift?

6. Which type of window or floor coverings would be easiest to maintain and healthy for your bathroom where water and mildew are constant threats to quality of the air and surfaces?

7. Would you like to try and use non-traditional furnishings such as sofas or chairs in a live-in bathroom type setting? Is this practical? Pay attention to the materials used, avoiding upholstered items unless they are covered with water-resistant fabrics.

Section 4

LIVING ROOMS

By tradition and architectural design, formal living rooms are usually the rooms we enter from the front door.

As the access point to the house, the living room readily presents itself for public display.

THIS IS THE SPACE—ALSO CALLED THE FRONT ROOM—that is usually the most "perfectly decorated," roped off (with furnishings sometimes under plastic), remaining vacuum-sealed until company comes.

But before you begin to outfit the living room, think about whether you'd like to live there. Perhaps you should bring it back to life by reconsidering how this room relates to your life and your home.

But even if the living room is where you spend a good deal of time, you should not ignore its special decorative needs and functions.

The options available for decorating in these public spaces may seem plentiful. The choices can be narrowed if you direct your decision-making according to the spatial, organizational and structural requirements of living that will take place in the room.

By looking at the common activities the living room must support, you may begin to understand what style of furniture, which types of fabrics and which window dressings will serve all the room's functions.

The decorative scheme you choose for your living room must be one with which you and your family feel comfortable. Successful rooms have a definite flavor (not to be confused with a "themed" look) that is expressed through its decorations. The living room is often defined by its largest piece of furniture, the sofa. But, as always, begin your decorating thoughts with the room itself and then everything else in relation to that.

If the goal for your living room is for social relaxation, then the furnishings should be of such shape and texture as to invite lingering and lounging.

If the living room's purpose is more of a family center where more than one activity is to take place—talking and viewing television, for example—you may want to pay special attention to how the furniture is positioned. Zones may be created within the living room—by careful placement of furniture—to facilitate many activities comfortably.

Comfort and ease of conversation were goals of this design, which includes lots of plump upholstery and furniture grouped for face-to-face meetings. INTERIOR DESIGN: ROBERT STILIN, INC.

Color directions

The direction the room faces may help
you to decide on a color scheme. North-
facing rooms receive fairly cold blue
light, and may benefit from warmer-
toned scheme in pinks, apricots, golds,
beiges or even reds, which will "warm"
the room. A west-facing or south-facing
room, which will be suffused with soft
golden light, can take cooler schemes.

A 1970s home with dark pine and post-and-beam construction was renovated into an airy contemporary residence highlighting expansive views of Colorado mountains. Evening sunsets cast blue and purple hues, inspiring the use of rich jewel tones against a light background. Interior Design: Sara Zook Designs Inc.

LIVING IN—AND WITH—YOUR LIVING ROOM

Take a closer look at your living room and its functions. Use these questions as a guide.

INTERIOR DESIGN: VAN MARTIN ROWE; PHOTO: TIM STREET-PORTER

1. Is your living room used only for guests or it is really a family room? Is it decorated or furnished to accommodate both family and visitors? How easily is it transformed from family to "company" space?

2. Is there a way to segregate the room to make it more "zoned" for use by those involved in many activities in the same space? Would simply re-arranging the furniture or moving the electronic entertainment center to a different location in the room create more of a village rather than a one-use space?

3. Are your furnishings comfortable and durable? Which fabrics might be better for upholstered items or would all wood furniture work better if you have pets or toddlers?

4. Is the living room a space that is under-used and would be better converted to office space or playspace? What furnishings could be better used in other areas of the house?

5. How "dated" does the carpeting or the wallcovering seem? Is there a simple fix-up in changing the color or the wallpaper design?

6. What's underfoot? What is the quality and appearance of the floor-covering, would adding area rugs or floorcloths, liven up the space?

7. Would slipcovers on the furniture make the space less formal when "company" or visitors are not being entertained? This essentially would give you two rooms—one for family fun and one for entertaining guests.

INTERIOR DESIGN: VAN MARTIN ROWE;
PHOTO: TIM STREET-PORTER

INTERIOR DESIGN: CONSTANCE GALLAGHER INTERIOR
DESIGN; PHOTO PETER JAQUITH

Section 5

DINING ROOMS

There are many who still find a dining room a necessary place for entertaining at home.

A separate room, away from the kitchen, allows dining in a relaxed, congenial environment.

For this reason, dining rooms are still given special decorating treatment as one of the more "public" rooms of the house.

IS THIS A SPACE FOR DINING IN TWICE A YEAR, or for full time use as a play area for youngsters?

Logical questions like this regarding the use of the dining room space in the modern home have been posed by home owners for the past three decades.

The revival of interest in in-kitchen eating and entertaining is sounding a death knell of sorts for the more formal dining space. Although quite a luxury if you have the space, the dining room in many modern homes now doubles as recreation or work space.

Decorating inspiration can derive from any source but most dining rooms tend to be put together to increase a mood of formality.

For this reason, historically, the color palettes of dining rooms have tended to be serious and dignified in character, with dark rather than lighter hues and furnishings of made of heavy, dark woods.

The decor of your dining room should reflect your style of entertaining. The choices of furnishings may seem obvious—a table and chairs—but you will want to pay much attention to the shape and materials of these furnishings.

Everything about your dining room will contribute to guests' expectations. Round tables, for example, tend to feel more "cozy" that oblong shapes. Round tables provide no natural "head," therefore make guests feel treated more democratically. But if you entertain more than six guests at a time, a rectangular table would be more efficient.

The center of the room is the accepted placement for tables and chairs, but examine your own space for possible variations. The center often wins out because it provides the best flow of traffic for guests and food service.

Remember that seating affects behavior, so you'll want your guest to rest nicely. Upholstered seating provides a place for lingering and more comfort during long meals. Less flexible, straight-backed chairs might be more suited to quick meals.

Dining rooms are becoming more informal affairs. In this room, classic seaside charm is enhanced with blue and white sunflower fabric-covered walls and a black Portuguese needlepoint rug underfoot. INTERIOR DESIGN: DIAMOND BARATTA DESIGN, INC.

A sideboard or console table, although not required, is a customary piece of furniture for a dining space and does provide storage and additional surface space for meal preparations.

Because of their location in a house's layout, usually between connecting rooms, dining rooms tend not to have heavy draperies or use fabric for decorative detail.

Special effects lighting, such as candles or overhead spots, should be used in dining areas, although most are illuminated by light from the hallways and surrounding rooms.

For a new look

Simple slipcovers can transform dining chairs into something else, at least temporarily. Using slipcovers, the chairs may be dressed up or down depending on the entertaining needs. Slipcovers usually have the advantage of being washable.

If you have the space and enjoy entertaining, a separate room for dining, apart from the cooking activities, is a luxury. Colors in formal dining spaces tend towards the darker hues to encourage a feeling of formality. Interior Design: J. Powell & Associates, Inc.

WHAT HAPPENS IN YOUR DINING ROOM?

Think about your dining room and what really works best in your home.

INTERIOR DESIGN: MANIJEH EMAY; PHOTO: STEVE VIERRA

1. What is the dining room used for? How often? Is that satisfying to you? How would you like for that to change?

2. Which activities could the room accommodate that the rest of your house does not? Is this where you should locate your home office? Should you consider dining room furniture that is movable so that during the day hours, for example, the space could be used as a play area or workspace or exercise space?

3. How useful is this room when not serving its primary function? Should you consider this space as a storage area?

4. What type of furniture for dining and eating do you now have? Is this conducive to the level of entertaining you now do? Would you like to entertain more in a formal setting? How can you make the space "grow" by making different choices in furniture—adding a large table, removing non-essential sideboards, etc.?

5. What other choices in wallcoverings, floor coverings and window dressings would lend the room the "feeling" you'd like for relaxed or more formal dining?

6. Would slipcovers on your dining chairs give you, in essence, two rooms. Dressed in slipcovers—that can be formal or informal—the dining space can become "themed" for any occasion or simply for visual variety.

INTERIOR DESIGN: ANNIE KELLY; PHOTO: TIM STREET-PORTER

Section 6

WORK SPACES

WORKING FROM HOME HAS BECOME A WAY OF LIFE for many in the past decade but often it is a luxury to find space at home for an "office."

Home offices tend to now be jerry-rigged someplace between the dining room and the garage, but there are some ways you might be able to set up shop.

Comfort, not decorative style, should influence your choices of furniture and furnishings for your work space.

For those who would be reassured by having an assigned place to work, the home office can be treated as one of the home's more formal rooms, with its own rules regarding access.

You may want to choose a space based not only on its size (and separation from the midst of domestic life) but also for the amount of natural light.

Ample sunlight and windows will limit the amount of artificial lighting you will have to introduce to make sure tasks are accomplished without eye strain.

Your furnishings need not come from the office supply store. Ideally, your workspace should reflect the rest of your home. A wonderful old pine table or antique desk could make a fine work station.

If you are housing a computer, make sure that the monitor, desk, chair and keyboard are adjusted to the correct ergonomic height for each user. Invest in a really good chair that offers easy flexibility in height.

You may also want to furnish your workspace with other, more relaxed seating in another area of the room to provide opportunities to step away from business for a moment.

Clutter never makes for productive space. Work spaces must be carefully planned to provide storage and working room. If your work involves a lot of papers and equipment, an efficient filing system is the first design consideration.

Use your wall space for storage. Wall-mounted shelving or filing systems might provide efficiency and free up floor space.

Some may not have the luxury of space for separating the work space, so some rooms—bedrooms and dining rooms—have to serve several purposes.

All things considered, your work space should be as inviting and functional as any other room in the house.

In selecting where a work station might be created in your home, ask yourself how much space and privacy is required.

The challenge of working in the home is keeping business and domestic life separate.

For privacy and to induce productivity, work spaces are ideally situated in low traffic parts of your home and where there is much natural light. INTERIOR DESIGN: CAROL R. KNOTT INTERIOR DESIGN

Now you see it, now you don't

- If you like the idea of keeping a handle on visual clutter but you must leave some work on your desk, consider desks with surface that be easily covered or that have rolling tops.
- Room dividers or screens of fabric or paper may be used to conceal unattractive office equipment when it is not in use.

To make your office feel like home

Equip your home office with convenience items such as a coffee maker and an electronic source of information. You might install a refrigerator or add plumbing, depending on your space and budget.

In these instances, in the bedroom, for example, you may be able to carve out a small niche for a compact unit. Keep your workstation near a window with your back to the bed, if possible, providing a different focal point for your work.

Work space in the dining room—usually on the table—presents the challenge of constantly having to put away the work. Perhaps a filing system (covered) may be incorporated into the room's furniture to accommodate this dual use.

If you need a work space but cannot get any from existing space, perhaps your office can be somewhat "virtual." Many office supply retailers offer compact, self-contained modular desks that can be folded down when not in use. You might also consider:

Flexible workstations: Purchase desk and filing units on casters that may be rolled or moved aside.

Hinged desktops: Tables attached to the walls—like those found in kitchen nooks—may be installed in placed where a surface is needed at times and can be raised and lowered according to need.

Tool sheds and other outdoor facilities: The space for your work may be outside of the home after all, even if only in the backyard. Prefabricated structures from tool sheds to covered gazebos may be fashioned into work spaces.

A functional space was carved from a corner of this family room. For efficiency, the monitor is recessed into the wall, the printer is closeted underneath, the computer and disks are in cabinets on the left, and the keyboard and mouse pad fold into drawers.

Interior design: Nancy Mullen, ASID, CKD; Photo: Richard Felber

THINK ABOUT THE OFFICE IN YOUR HOME

INTERIOR DESIGN: PAMELA KARLYN MAZOW; PHOTO: PETER JAQUITH

1. Do you need a home office? Why?

2. What space do you have available for conversion into a work-space? Is there some place in the exterior of your home that might work better? A shed in the backyard, for example?

3. Must this workspace accommodate one or many people? What are the tasks those individuals are trying to perform?

4. Are there special seating and desk arrangements needed for efficient work? Drafters and artists might not need a desk but rather a large work table. What type of furniture do you need?

5. What type of access do you need to telephone lines or computer hook-ups? Is there also a need for entertainment centers—VCRs, radios, etc?

6. How much privacy is required? Should you consider room dividers as part of your choices of workspace furniture? Do you need to consider seating or lounging furniture for those moments of relaxed contemplation? How much furniture can you live without in this space to make room for storage devices?

7. Have you considered the storage needs and future growth needs in the overall design and furniture selections?

8. What have you done about the ambiance and lighting? Is it suitable and conducive to productive work?

Use these pages of graph paper to create a floor plan your home.

Directory of Designers/ Manufacturers/ Retailers

Anjum Razvi, ASID
Razvi Design Studio
14829 Pensaquitos
Court
San Diego, CA 92129
858/672.8831

Ann Lenox
13279 Vinter Way
Poway, CA 92064-1216
858/673.7184

**Ann Sacks Tile
and Stone**
8120 N.E. 33rd Drive
Portland, OR 97211
503/280.9701
Fax: 503/331.7330

Annie Kelly
2074 Watsonia Terrace
Los Angeles, CA 90068

Antine Associates
1028 Arcadian Way
Fort Lee, NJ 07024
201/941.8048

**Arthur de Mattos Casas
Studio Arthur de
Mattos Casas**
Alameda Ministro
Rocha Azevedo/052
Sao Paulo, Brazil
CEP 01410002
011-55-11-282-6311

Artistic Tile
Mullica Hill, NJ
856/464.8795

**Austin Patterson
Disston**
376 Pequot Avenue
Southport, CT 06490
203/255.4031
Fax: 203/254.1390

**Barbara Colman
Covington/Colman**
14 Imperial Place
Providence, RI
Covington 02903

Bardelli
(see Italian Tile)

**Barry Brukoff
Brukoff Design
Associates**
480 Gate Five Road
Sausalito, CA 94965
415/332.6350
Fax: 415/332.5968

Benjamin Noriega-Ortiz
75 Spring Street
New York, NY 10012
212/343.9709
Fax: 212/343.9263

**Bierly-Drake &
Associates**
17 Arlington Street
Boston, MA 02116
617/247.0081

Bisazza
8530 N.W. 30th Terrace
Miami, FL 33122
305/597.4090

**Bisazza, North
American Showroom**
12 W. 24th Street
New York, NY 10010
212/463.0620

Blair Associates
315 West 78th Street
New York, NY 10024
212/595.0203

Brenda Lanza
13279 Vinter Way
Poway, CA 92064
858/673.7184

**Brian Murphy
BAM Design**
150 W. Channel Road
Santa Monica, CA
90404
310/459.0955

Brunschwig & Fils
979 Third Avenue
New York, NY
10022-1234
212/838.7878
Fax: 212/371.3026

C. Weaks Interiors, Inc.
3133 Maple Drive
Suite 150
Atlanta, Georgia 30305
404/233.6040
Fax: 404/233.6043

California Art Tile
(see Kohler)

Cann & Company
450 Harrison Avenue
Boston, MA 02118

**Carol Conway Design
Association**
8242 E. Del Codena
Scottsdale, AZ 85258
408/948.1959
Fax: 408/948.1959

Carol G. Brown, ASID
7541 Eads Avenue
La Jolla, CA 92037
858/551.8143

**Carol Helms,
Garden Design
Magazine Meigher
Communications**
666 Sixth Avenue
New York, NY 10013
212/219.7472

**Carol R. Knott
Interior Design**
430 Green Bay Road
Kenilworth, IL 60043
857/256.6676

**Carrie Brockman's
Design Group**
770 Forsyth 2nd floor
Clayton, MO 63105
314/726.6333
Fax: 314/726.0522
www.carriebrockman.com

**Ceramica Bechinense,
S.A. Cerabec**
Camino de la Mina, s/n
BECHI(Castellon)12549
Spain 964/620400
Fax: 964/621213

Cerasarda
(see Italian Tile)

**Chambers Interiors and
Associates, Inc.**
2719 Vaclede, Suite B
Dallas, TX 75204
214/651.7665

Charles Riley
45 Fifth Avenue
New York, NY 10003

**Charlotte S. Jensen,
FASID**
11464 Escoba Place
San Diego, CA
92127-1015
858/693.9294
Fax: 858/487.6895

Christian Liaigre
61 rue de Varenne
Paris, France 75007

**Christine Brun Abnelnour
Christine Brun &
Associates**
7541 Eads Avenue, #A
La Jolla, CA 92037
619/551.9601

**Contance Gallagher
Interior Design**
11 Adams Street
Charlestown, MA 02129
617/242.0266

Crate & Barrel
725 Landwehr Road
Northbrook, IL 60062
847/272.2888
Fax: 847/272.2938

**Dawn Southworth &
Dana Salvo**
63 Bennett Street
Gloucester, MA 01930
978/283.9638

Decorating Den Interiors
19100 Montgomery
Village Avenue,
Montgomery Village,
MD 20886
800/332.3367
Fax: 301/272.1520
www.decoratingden.com

Deutsch/Parker
Design, Ltd.
1240 N. Lakeshore
Drive
Apt. 31 B
Chicago, IL 60610
312/ 595.9330

Diamond Baratta
Design, Inc.
270 Lafayette Street
New York, NY 10012
212/966.8892
Fax: 212/966.4261

Diane Harsch
Emphasis Planning
& Design
2194 Carmel Valley Rd.
Del Mar, CA 92014
858/259.8892
Fax: 858/259.0297

Diane Wendell
Interior Design
1121 Warren Avenue
Downers Grove, IL
60515
630/988.8341

Domain Home
Furnishings
7 Newbury Street
Boston, MA 02116
617/266.5252

Doree Friedman
1615 Cortland Street
San Francisco, CA
94110
415/487.1857

Eduardo Souto Moura
Souto Moura -
Arquitectos, Lda.
Rua do Aleixo, 53
4150
Porto Portugal

Elizabeth Read Weber
Elizabeth Read Interiors
79 East Putnam Avenue
Greenwich, CT 06830
203/869.5659
Fax: 203/869.3778

Mark Enos
Enos & Co.
705 N. Alfred Street
Los Angeles, CA 90069
323/655.0109
Fax: 323/655.7719

Environments by
Marilyn Frances Lundy
One Lincoln Plaza,
Suite 305
New York, NY 10023
212/362 7057
Fax: 212/362.7057

Est Est, Inc.
North Pacesetter Way
Scottsdale, AZ 85251
480/563.1555

FSC Wallcoverings
Division of Schumacher
& Co. (See Schumacher
& Co.)

Fired Earth
Thyford Mill, Oxford Rd
Adderbury, Oxon
0X17 3HP
44 01295 812088

Fu Tung Cheng
Cheng Design
2808 San Pablo Avenue
Berkeley, CA 94702
510/849.3272
Fax: 510/549.2821

Gail Adams
Interiors Ltd.
110 East San Miguel
Phoenix, AZ 85012
602/274.0074

Gayle Shaw Camden
552 Rivard Boulevard
Grosse Point, MI 48230
313/885.0767

Gramercy
79 Madison Avenue
New York, NY 10016
212/213.7795

Gustavson
192 Lexington Avenue
Suite 801
New York, NY 10016

Harlequin
5100 Highlands
Parkway
Smyrna, GA 30082
888/326.4234

Horne International
Designs, Inc.
5272 River Road,
Suite 450
Bethesda, MD 20816
301/656.4304
Fax: 301/907.0258

ICT, Inc.
RT 1, Box 209
Coupland, TX 78615
512/285.5841
Fax: 512/285.5393

Il Pavone
(see Italian Tile)

Illahe Tileworks
Susan Werschkul,
Design
695 Mistletoe Road, #F,
Ashland, OR 97520
541/488.5072

Imperial Home Decor
23645 Mercantile Road
Beechwood, OH 44122
216/464.3700

Insight West
Bruce Goers,
Wayne Williamson
& Sam Cardella
45-125 Panorama Dr.
Palm Desert, CA 92260
760/568.9089

Italian Tile: Italian
Trade Commission
- Bardelli, through
  Hastings Tile
- Cerasarda, through
  Ex, Inc.

- Il Pavone, through
  Artistic Tile
499 Park Avenue
New York, NY 10022
212/758.1050

J. Powell and
Associates, Inc.
100 W. Beaver Creek
Boulevard
P.O. Box 1641
Avon, CO 81620
970/845.7731
Fax: 970/845.8903

Jackie Naylor
Interiors, Inc.
4287 Glengary Drive
Atlanta, GA 30342
404/814.1973
Fax: 404/814.1973

James R. Irving, ASID
13901 Shaker
Boulevard
Cleveland, OH 44120
216/283.1991
or 216/751.1100

Jane J. Marsden
Antiques &
Interiors, Inc.
2300 Peachtree Road,
102A
Atlanta, GA 30309
404/355.1288
Fax: 404/355.4552

Kar Ho Architects
117 West 17th Street
New York, NY 10011
212/237.3450

Kathleen M.
Zbacnik, ASID
7556 Fay Avenue
La Jolla, CA 92037
858/454.8090

Kelly Wearstler
KWID
113 1/2 N.
La Brea Avenue
Los Angeles, CA 90036
323/931.8061

Ken Kelleher
30 Ipswich Street #305
Boston, MA 02215
617/262.2060

Kentucky Wood Floors
P.O. Box 33276
Louisville, KY 40232
502/451.6024
Fax: 502/451.6027

Klingmans
Furniture Company
3525 28th Street S.E.
Grand Rapids, MI
49512
616/942.7300
Fax: 616/942.1957

Kohler Company
444 Highland Drive
Kohler, WI 53044
920/457.4441

Kuckly Associates
506 E. 74th Street
New York, NY 10021
212/772.2228
Fax: 212/772.2130

Laura Birns, ASID
P.O. Box 812
Del Mar, CA 92014
858/259.0750

Leslie Jones, Inc.
754 N. Milwaukee
Avenue
Chicago, IL 60622
312/455.1147
Fax: 312/455.1264

Letelier & Rock
Design, Inc.
1020 Madison
New York City, NY
10021
212/683.5512
Fax: 212/683.7608

Leavitt/Weaver, Inc.
451 Tully Road
Modesto, CA 95350
209/521.5125

Lillian Bogossian
and Vivian Weil
Decorative Interiors
162 Elm Street
Manchester Center, VT
05255
802/362.4836

Linda Medina, ASID
3255 Talbot Street
San Diego, CA 92106
619/226.8483

Lise Davis Interiors
14 Acorn Street
Boston, MA 02108
617/367.9533

Lloy Hack Associates
425 Boylston Street
Boston, MA 02116
617/247.8835

Manijeh Emay
M.M. Interiors
P.O. Box 160
Osterville, MA 02655
508/428.4966

Manuel de
Santaren, Inc.
Interior Decoration
& Design
One Design Center Place
Suite 44
Boston, MA 02210
617/330.6998
Fax: 617/330.7980

Marcia Connors
& Roxy Gray
Growing Space
Interior Design
4 Fall Lane
Canton, MA 02021
781/575.1991

Marian Glasgow
Interiors
9 Laurel Street
Newton Centre, MA
01776
617/965.0936

Mark Enos
Enos & Co.
705 North Alfred Street
Los Angeles, CA 90069
323/635.0109
Fax: 323/655.7719

Marsha Sewell, ASID
629 5th Avenue
San Diego, CA 92101
619/696.7575

Mary W. Delaney
Interior Design
1 Strawberry Hill Court
Stamford, CT 06902
203/348.6839
Fax: 203/324.7229

MaryClare Brandt, ASID
MC Brandt Interior Design
San Diego, CA 92101
858/453.8278

Marylin Matson
The J.H. Wolfe
Company, Inc.
833-A South Main Street
#396
Fallbrook, CA 92028

Meadowbank
Design Inc.
Box 168
Bryn Mawr, PA 19010
610/525.4909
Fax: 610/525.3909

Michael C.F. Chan
& Associates, Inc.
3550 W. 6th Street, PH
Los Angeles, CA 90020
213/383.2162
Fax: 213/383.1815

Michael de Santis, Inc.
1110 Second Avenue
New York, NY 10022

Michael R. Golden
Design
37 West 20th Street
New York, NY 10001
212/645.3001
Fax: 212/645.3003

Milling Road,
A Division of Baker
Furniture
329 N. Hamilton
High Point, NC 27260
336/885.1800
Fax: 336/885.1825

Nancy Mullen,
ASID, CKD
NDM Kitchens, Inc.
204 E. 77th Street
New York, NY 10021
212/628.4629
Fax: 212/628.6738

Noha & Associates
1735 W. Fletcher
Chicago, IL 60657
773/549.1414
Fax: 773/549.1479

Olson Lewis &
Dioli Architects
17 Elm Street
Manchester-by-the-Sea,
MA 01944
978/526.4386

Pacific Design Center
(see Kohler)

Paul Magnuson
10 Central Street
Beverly, MA 01915

Peter Forbes
and Associates
70 Long Wharf
Boston, MA 02110
617/523.5800
Fax: 617/523.5810

Poliform USA, Inc.
150 East 58th Street,
Floor 9
New York, NY 10155

Raymond Joseph
1901 West Race Street
Chicago, IL 60622
312/733.2312

Rita St. Clair
Associates, Inc.
1009 N. Charles Street
Baltimore, MD 21201
410/752.1313
Fax: 410/752.1335

Robert Stilin, Inc.
P.O. Box 4189
East Hampton, NY
11937
631/537.7236

Sanderson & Son
285 Grand Avenue
3 Patriot Center
Englewood, NJ 07631
201/894.8400
Fax: 201/894.8871

Sandra Nunnerly, Inc.
595 Madison Avenue
New York, NY 10022
212/826.0539
Fax: 212/826.1146

Sara Zook Designs
3700 Havana Street #214
Denver, CO 80239
303/237.4544
Fax: 303/237.1647

Schumacher
79 Madison Avenue
New York, NY 10016
800/988.7775
Fax: 212/213.7848
Email: consumer@fsco.com
www.fsco.com

Seabrook Wallcoverings
1325 Farmville Road
Memphis, TN 38122
800/238.9152
Fax: 901/320.3675

Searl Design
808 Garnet Circle
Fort Lauderdale, FL 33326
954/349.1005

Sistine Interiors
1359 North Beverly Drive
Beverly Hills, CA 90210
310/246.1888
Fax: 310/246.1889

Soikkeli & Company
P.O. Box 1195
Vineyard Haven, MA 02568
508/693.9359

Stedila Design
135 E. 55th Street
New York City, NY 10022
212/751.4281
Fax: 212/751.6698

Sunworthy Wallcoverings
195 Walker Drive
Brampton, Ontario
Canada LGT 3Z9
905/791.8788
Fax: 905/790.4883
www.sunworthy.com

Susan Baker
(see ICT, Inc.)

Susan Lefkowitz
13279 Vinter Way
Poway, CA 92064-1216
858/673.7184

**Suzanne McCallen/
G.S. Hinsen Company**
2133 Bandywood
Nashville, TN 37215
615/383.6440
Fax: 615/269.5130

Talavera de Mexico
(see ICT, Inc.)
011 52 418 24761

**Tangee Harris-Prichett
Tangee, Inc.**
5306 South Hyde Park
Boulevard
Chicago, IL 60615
773/955.5175
Fax: 773/955.5196

**Tile by Design
Nan Owen**
24291 Sunnybrook Circle
Lake Forest, CA 92630
949/855.7877

Tomar Lampert Associates
8900 Melrose Avenue,
Suite 202
Los Angeles, CA 90069
310/271.4299
Fax: 310/271.1569

Trilogy
Village Green
Bedford, NY 10506
914/234.3071
Fax: 914/234.0540

Van Martin Rowe
East Colorado Boulevard
Pasadena, CA 91107
626/577.4736

**Vicente Wolf
Associates, Inc.**
333 West 39th Street
New York, NY 10018
212/465.0590
Fax: 212/465.0639

**Village Consumer
Referral Service**
79 Madison Avenue
New York, NY 10016
800/552.WALL
Fax: 212/213.7640

Walker Design Group
7125 E. 2nd Street, #103
Scottsdale, AZ 85251
480/945.1460
Fax: 480/945.1322

Walker Zanger
8901 Bradley Avenue
Sun Valley, CA 91001
818/504.0235

Waterworks
29 Park Avenue
Danbury, CT 06810
800/899.6757

Wood-Mode, Inc.
One Second Street
Kreamer, PA 17833
570/374.2711
Fax: 570/372.1422

York Wallcoverings
750 Linden Avenue
P.O. Box 5166
York, PA 17405-5166
717/846.4456
Fax: 717/843.5624
International Fax:
717/843.8167

Directory of Photographers

Jaime Ardiles-Arce
730 Fifth Avenue
New York, NY 1019
212/333.8779 or
212/371.4949

**Bjorg Arnarsdottir
Twist Visuals, Inc.**
447 Fort Washington #61
New York, NY 10033
212/740.6310
Email:bjorg@
bjorg@bjorgphoto.com
www.bjorgphoto.com

Andre Baranowski
101 Old Mamaroneck Road
Suite 2B2
White Plains, NY 10605
914/948.6261

**Patricia Bean
Graphic Photography**
3626 Ross Lane
Central Point, OR 97502
541/732.0643

Robert Benson
140 Huyshop Avenue 5J
Hartford, CT 06106
860/724.2939

**Tony Berardi
Photofields**
36W830 Stonebridge
Lane Street
St. Charles, IL 60175
603/587.5530
Fax: 630/584.8035

Hedrich Blessing
11 West Illinois Street
Chicago, IL 60610
312/321.1151
Fax: 312/321.1165

Mark Boisclair
5804 East Sandra Terrace
Phoenix, AZ
602/957.6997

**Jim Brady
Brady Architectural
Photography**
1010 University Avenue,
#823
San Diego, CA 92103
619/296.5304
Fax: 619/296.5304

Kim Brun Studios
9605 S.W. Ventura Court
Tigard, OR 97223
503/977.9502

Coll Photography
1715 9th Street
Berkeley, CA 94710
510/526.2539
Fax: 510/526.2539
Email: beacoll@sirius.com
www.collphotography.com

Grey Crawford
101 N. Grand Avenue
#21
Pasadena, CA 91103
626/304.2646
Fax: 626/304.2648

Stephen Cridland
1231 N. W. Hoyt, #306
Portland, OR 97209
503/274.0954
Fax: 503/274.1247
scrid@teleport.com
www.stevecridland.com

Jacques Dirand
10 Pessage Doisy
75017
Paris, France
0145 74 1164
Fax: 0140 68 9995

**Philip H. Ennis
Photography**
114 Millertown Road
Bedford, NY 10506
914/234.9574
Fax: 914/234.0360

Richard Felber
8 Ore Hill Road
Kent, CT 06757
860/927.4016

Luis Ferreira-Alves
Rua de Alegria
Parque Habitacional
do Lima
Entrada 29
Habitacao 3A Porto
Portugal

David Glomb
71340 Estellita Drive
Rancho Mirage, CA
92270
760/340.4455
Fax: 760/779.1872

Ed Gohlich
P.O. 180919
Coronado, CA 92178
619/423.4237
Fax: 619/423.4233

Sam Gray
844 Summer Street
Boston, MA 02127
617/269.9620
Fax:617/269.2507
sgp@samgray.com
www.samgray.com

John M. Hall
500 West 58th Street,
3F
New York, NY 10019
212/757.0369
Fax: 212/956.1462

Peter Jaquith
6 Pleasant Street
Beverly, MA 01915
978/921.4737
Fax: 978/969.1737

**Charlotte S. Jensen,
FASID**
11464 Escoba Place
San Diego, CA 92127-
1015
858/693.9294
Fax: 858/487.6895

Balthazar Korab Ltd.
P.O. Box 895
Troy, MI 48099
248/641.8881
Fax: 248/641.8889

Tim Lee Photography
2 Zachary Lane
New Milford, CT 06776
860/355.4661
Fax: 860/350.3526
tim@timleephoto.com
www.timleephoto.com

Peter Margonelli
20 Debrosses Street
New York, NY
10013-1704
212/941.0380
Fax: 212/334.4449

Jeff McNamara
68 Vista
Easton, CT 06612
203/459.9175

John Miller
11 West Illinois Street
Chicago, IL 60610
312/321.1151
Fax: 312/321.1165

Leonard Mysynski
2229 Elden Ave/Suite D
Costa Mesa, CA 92627
949/645.3388
Fax: 949/515.5146
lmysz@earthlink.net

Mary E. Nichols
232 North Arden
Boulevard
Los Angeles, CA 90001
323/871.0770
Fax: 323/871.0775

Ira Nowinski
10 Allen Court
San Rafael, CA 94901
412/495.6865
Fax: 415/485.1650

**Peter Paige
Photography**
7 Sunset Lane
Upper Saddle River, NJ
07458
201/236.8730
Fax: 201/236.8732

Carol Peerce
2870 5th Avenue
Suite #103
San Diego, CA 92103
619/297.4773
Fax: 619/297.4783
cpphish@aol.com
www.peerce.com

Robert Perron
119 Chestnut Street
Branford, CT 06405
203/481.2004
Fax: 203/481.5041
www.bobperron.com

Dorothy Perry
2124 Whipple
Chicago, IL 60647
773/278.5446

Eric Roth
P.O. Box 422
Topsfield, MA 01983
978/887.1975
Fax: 978/887.5035
www.ericrothphoto.com

Tim Street-Porter
2074 Watsonia Terrace
Los Angeles, CA 90068
323/874.4278

Steve Vierra
P.O. Box 1827
Sandwich, MA 02563
508/477.7043
Fax: 508/833.0795
vierraphoto@aol.com

Alan Weintraub
1832A Mason Street
San Francisco, CA
94133
415/553.8191
Fax: 415/553.8192

Index of Designers/ Manufacturers/ Retailers

Index of Photographers